AF440712

# The Time for Revolution Is Now!

## A Social History of Trans and Travesti Argentina

All the illustrations in this book are courtesy of the Mariano Moreno National Library (Argentina). Archives Department. Sarmiento Publishing Collection. Crónica Editorial Archive.

ISBN: 979-8-234-08038-7

Printed in the United States of America

# The Time for Revolution Is Now!

## A Social History of Trans and Travesti Argentina

Marce Joan Butierrez

# Contents

# List of Illustrations

*The Time of Revolution is Now!*

# Acknowledgments

This book is the result of the collective efforts of colleagues and friends dedicated to the vital work of constructing and preserving trans and queer archives. I am deeply grateful to the Department of Archives and Special Collections at the National Library *Mariano Moreno,* the "Sex and Revolution" Program at the Center of Documentation on Leftist Culture and Politics (CeDInCI), and *Archivos Desviados.*

I also wish to recognize the editorial support of the LatFem team, specifically Vanina Escales, Anuka Fernández Fuks, and María Mariasch, as well as the editors of *Moléculas Malucas*: Mabel Bellucci, Marcelo Ernesto Ferreyra, and Juan Queiroz.

Most importantly, these articles would not exist without the inspiration and resilience of my travesti and transsexual friends. Every message, conversation, and shared story has shaped the person I am today. I am especially indebted to the friendship of Julieta *"La Trachyn"* Gonzalez and Karina Urbina, as well as Perica, Mary, Vicky, Casandra, Sandy, Alma, Rosario, Caro, Marzia, and all my trans accomplices in this journey.

Finally, my deepest thanks to my best friend, Mir Yarfitz, for standing by me and encouraging my dreams, and to James L. Richie IV, for teaching me that I am worthy of love.

# Introduction

Over the past decade, I have researched diverse travesti experiences in Argentina, primarily from a historical perspective. I have also documented mobility practices and political initiatives. Much of my work has been published in academic papers, some of which have been published in English. Since 2019, however, I have worked as a journalist for some of the most prominent feminist and LGBTQ+ magazines, digital outlets, and newspapers in Argentina. I began writing weekly articles and op-eds for media outlets because I felt a social responsibility to share my research beyond the often strict limits of academia. I gradually became acquainted with the English-speaking world dedicated to trans studies and noticed the lack of representation of travesti experiences outside of South America. In fact, even among Latin American specialists, the main focus is Mexico and the Caribbean, with Brazil receiving little attention. This is why I started participating in conferences, meetings, journals, and workshops in the United States and Europe with friends and colleagues. A few years ago, I moved to Michigan, which transformed my personal life and professional goals. Today, I work as a journalist in the United States, and I will soon start my Ph.D. program at the University of Minnesota, which is one of my biggest dreams.

One of the main questions this book attempts to answer is why translating South American travesti experiences into English is important. My best friend and colleague, Mir Yarfitz, and I published a challenging article in the Oxford

Research Encyclopedia of Latin American History about trans and travesti identities in twentieth-century South America (Butierrez and Yarfitz 2024). In the article, Mir and I compile a significant amount of information about trans and travesti identities across the region. We attempt to connect certain experiences while highlighting the unique characteristics of others. Despite the significant effort in the article, it remains challenging to disseminate travesti experiences beyond academic circles. Even among trans scholars, the few mentions of travesti identity are inaccurate, as they consider it only as a recent political statement under the decolonizing practice of trans activism in the region. Others only pay attention to travesti identity as a theatrical practice, translating it as 'transvestite' or 'cross-dresser.' However, travesti is not the same as transvestite. Although it is sometimes considered a theatrical practice in some Latin American countries, it is not comparable to drag queen or cross-dressing experiences. Travesti identity has particularities that I discuss in depth in the articles included in this book. Mainly, it is an experience linked with eroticism, sex work, the marginalized condition of the working class in the region, and a strong political rhetoric embodied in the flesh and silicone of travesti people.

In Argentina, the term "*travesti*" originated in theatrical performances featuring men dressed as women. It gained popularity following the visit of a Brazilian travesti troupe in 1971. Was the term "*travesti*" used in Argentina before that date? Yes, of course. The social practice of living dressed as women has existed for many years, but it has taken different forms throughout history. In Brazil, the term used for this practice was "*travesti*," which literally means "*transvestite*" in Portuguese and other Romance languages, such as French (Kulick 1998). Brazil is the  origin of the word, but all South American countries had a social practice related to wearing clothes of the opposite sex. In Peru, documents and drawings from colonial times testify to the existence of "*travestis*" (Henderson 2012). In Bolivia, men wearing women's clothing participated in carnival celebrations as part of a ritual and theatrical parade (Aruquipa Pérez 2016). Perhaps some of them also identified with the opposite sex. Similar examples exist in each country. Despite the lack of documentation on these practices, it is possible to find documentation against the travesti practice. Throughout the continent, each national government created laws and ordinances to ban, persecute, and incarcerate people who wore clothes contrary to the sex assigned at birth.

Although its origins are linked with the theatrical practice, travesti became a word used by the popular press and the society to name any experience related with men who wear feminine clothes. After its most prolific time in the 1970s when many travesti groups traveled across South America performing their shows, during the large wave of military dictatorships in the region the travestis sought refuge in brothels and cabarets in the outskirts of the main cities. These places were a mix of show and sex work. Travestis often started out working as sex workers rather than as theatre performers. In the 1980s, with the diffusion of silicone injections travestis achieved a kind of corporality, curvy and sexy, that captured the attention of the press and media. Travestis used the media outlet to spread their discontent with the social violence, discrimination, and police repression. They constituted the first assemblies and political organizations and developed a complex narrative articulating the debates about sex, gender, and social class. Today, travesti identity is more than a label to describe a social and sexual practice, it is also a political statement against the binarism and rules that regulate gender.

Although for many authors the travesti experience is considered untranslatable I find many connections between the South America travesti experience and some documented activism in the United States that could enable a translation. The influence is pretty obvious. The United States received a large number of Latin American immigrants during the last century, therefore it is not hard to find expression of Latin experiences in this country. Among them, the most important from my perspective was the activism of Marsha P. Johnson and Sylvia Rivera, leaders of S.T.A.R Street Transvestites Action Revolutionaries (Rivera and Johnson 2013). Marsha P. Johnson, but more strongly Sylvia Rivera, embodied a kind of activism in defense of street transvestites that mixed the awareness about gender with a narrative about the class inequalities and social justice that I could compare with the political structure of travesti activism in South America. For the moment, I will use the term travesti in Spanish following the current tendency in the field, but in the future the next generation of trans scholars should connect the travesti and street transvestite experiences in a broader perspective about class and gender. I hope this book promotes this perspective still unexplored in trans studies, and especially important in this time of growing fascism and degradation of social marginalized communities around the globe.

The articles compiled in this book were originally published in Spanish between 2020 and 2024. During this 4-years period I collaborated with the most important blogs, newspapers and magazines about LGBT and feminism issues in Argentina. Most of these articles were published in LatFem, a digital media outlet founded in 2016 during the first feminist demonstrations against feminicides in Argentina. "Ni *una menos*" [Not one less] was the name of a big demonstration organized by feminist journalists in 2016, similar to the global experience of Me Too. LatFem emerged during that event as a criticism against the lack of feminist voices in the media. As a journalist I found in LatFem an incredible group of colleagues and friends that always supported my ideas and encouraged me to  write from my often pessimistic perspective about the trans and travesti experiences in Argentina. As part of my job in LatFem y reported about the conquest of the Trans Employment Quota Law, the first national census with non-binary categories, and the decree that established the non-binary ID's cards in Argentina.

In this book I also included articles originally published in Moleculas Malucas, a blog about queer archives and history coordinated by Mabel Belluci, Marcelo Ferreyra, and Juan Queiroz. Moleculas was an amazing adventure, led by three of the most incredible archivists and historians on trans and queer issues in Argentina. The mission of the blog was to highlight the history of trans and queer communities with the particular style of trans and queer historians that work with archives. I published my three most important research articles in Moleculas, and all of them are included in this book, this time translated into English. In addition I included in the book some essays, conference presentations, and articles never published before or distributed only as a draft among colleagues and friends. These articles cover a large diversity of topics, events and stories of trans and travesti people in Argentina and the region that I organize under four topic sections.

The first section is about the history of trans and travesti activism in Argentina. I included four articles in this section, two of them published in non-academic context where I explored the notion of travesti fury, a term invented by Lohana Berkins that symbolizes the key aspects of travesti political experiences. I also included the translation of an academic article published as part of a book collecting the experiences of trans activism in the 20th century and an essay about the links between travesti activism and sex work, during the 80s and 90s, based on interviews and documents. This section aims to analyze the complexity of travesti activism, sometimes reduced to an imitative experience of queer activism in the global north.

The second section is also about trans and travesti activism but more specifically about the connections between these experiences and the activism for human rights in Argentina. Human Rights organizations in Argentina have played a key role in the political narratives of the last two decades, because the memory about the last dictatorship, the struggle for justice, and the seeking of the disappeared people and their children and grandchildren are the core of political life since the return to democracy in 1983. Trans and travesti activism developed a complex relation with the corpus of memories about the last dictatorship, demanded recognition and reparatory policies, and articulated their demands in the same argumentative line of human rights organizations. One of the main results of this link was the numerous trans and travesti archives that emerged during the last decade, mostly oriented to produce evidence and social impact in favor of trans and travesti people who suffered incarceration and repression by the military junta between 1974 to 1983. This section contains four articles with different perspectives about the topic, two of them are focused on the travesti experience and their testimonies about the last dictatorship. These articles are the result of interviews and reports from a journalistic perspective, where the travesti voices are highlighted in order to recognize their struggle for recognition and reparation. I also included two articles written for journals and conferences with a more critical perspective about the topic, regarding the work of colleagues who, like me, propose a more broadly analysis of the violence against trans and queer people independently of the political violence during the last military dictatorship in Argentina.

The third section includes articles with a more biographical style, focused mainly on the activism of Karina Urbina and Pelusa Liendro, and some other activists. These two leaders were mostly underrepresented, as well as the transsexual and travesti sex work experience in Argentina. These four articles aim to highlight experiences that do no fit in the mainstream narrative against sex work or focused on travesti lives. Karina was one of the main transsexual activists and she embodied the voice of a generation of transsexuals worried about the prohibition of access to sex change surgeries in Argentina. Not necessarily in Karina's discourse, but in most of the transsexual testimonies in the 90s they declared to be born in a 'wrong body,' but this narrative is today mostly rejected in feminist, trans and queer worlds. The first article plays with Beauvoir's notion of 'no one born women' to discuss how the transsexual rhetoric was articulated around some ideas about femininity today under controversy. I also developed the history of some travesti sex workers that were forbidden because of their controversial misbehavior, their link with the sexual work, and their disobedient voices. Finally, the fourth section is a short collection of articles about the recent events in Argentina trans and queer context. I especially covered some significant events like the enactment of the trans labor quota act, the debates about the first census that registered non-binary identities, the achievement of legal abortion in Argentina, and some debates on the LGBT political horizons. The last article, never published before, is a crude text about my own discomfort with the new LGBT political organizations and the celebration of some 'queer perspectives' that only reinforce the power of capitalism in our own community.

This book is a collection of ideas and reflections on the history of trans people in Argentina and South America. It is also a collection of stories about my close friends who inspired my research and who have experienced violence at the hands of the Argentine government, police, and military forces over the last 100 years. The title of this book reflects the legacy of Lohana Berkins, who wrote in her final letter before her death:

> We have achieved many victories over the years. Now is the time to resist and fight for their continuity. **The time for revolution is now** because we will never return to prison. I am convinced that love is the engine of change.

As one of the few travesti scholars in Argentina I agree with Lohana 100%: We, the trans and travesti community, have achieved great things in the last decade. Now is the time to defend all our conquests and imagine a new horizon for our political struggle. This book showcases the experiences, stories, memories, and testimonies of our South American trans ancestors as tools for building a better future for the next generation of trans activists.

One of the main reasons, perhaps the main reason, why I published this book is because I believe in the power of history as a weapon for revolution and social change.

Edward Palmer Thompson (1980) says: *History is a cultural form within which we fight and many have fought before us. Nor are we alone when we fight there for we are historians because we know that the past is not dead, inert, and confining, but is strong with energies which can brought once again to our side.* My deeper desire is that this book brought our community and the generation before us the energy to fight and pursue a better world for everyone. For many years, our history was written by cis people, distorted under the political agenda of cis people, and used for individual interest. My generation grew up under  prejudices like 'all the trans women have HIV,' 'the life expectancy of trans people is 35 years,' and 'no man will ever love you.' If I had let these ideas grow on my mind, probably this book would never exist. I used History as a tool for my own revolution. I took the stories of my friends  to give hope myself, to keep myself in the battle against fear, to pursue love. Now I can share those stories with readers and teach them about our history, so that everyone who is tired of fighting knows: you're not alone anymore.

# Historicizing Trans and Travesti Activism

# A Travesti Odyssey: Traveling Across the Universe of Lohana Berkins

When embarking on a journey, every culture has its traditions and talismans. Sometimes, a mother's blessing and a few hugs serve as a talisman against all adversity. Today I am setting out on a journey, and Lohana is protecting me during this experience: two magazines that were published the week she passed away and that, for some reason, let's call it fate, found their way back into my hands as I was packing my bags. On the left margin of the cover of a newspaper titled *En nuestras voces* [In Our Voices], Lohana's brown face blends into a gray background, and her gaze, lost in the sky, contains a spark that seems to fade behind the horizon. A priori, I think of that version of Lohana who, tired of pretending to speak in a girly voice, decided to fearlessly embrace her loud travesti voice. A voice that was heard louder than ever. In an inexplicable sob, I left the magazines among the pile of essential papers and ran off to cry. I never met Berkins in person, but in the tears of those of us who emigrated, there is always a warm comfort when we remember her voice.

The purpose of this article is to reflect on her legacy beyond anecdotes and highlight some of the lessons Berkins taught us. Perhaps between one idea and another we will shed a tear or let out a laugh, but there is no other way to navigate trans lives than by producing theory, humor, and political praxis at the same time. Everything that seems easily locatable on binary categories for cis people, is tinged and confused for us like a pile of feathers on a carnival costume[1]. Lohana was always mutanting, she was always in the gerund form: she was being, doing, saying, living. Any label was tight and uncomfortable for her. That is why, in order to understand her, we need her voice, her unapologetic and undisguised voice, capable of saying the funniest and most bitter things in the same sentence. And we need to keep our ears open and our minds ready to understand that multiple forms of life inhabit the porous territories of sexualities.

If we were to consider a travesti theory of Lohana Berkins, we would have to look at words, the pen, and the fist at the same time, because a travesti theory is inevitably a way of intervening, embodying, and explaining the world. Nothing Lohana said in her thousands of interviews is just a random expression; every word is intersected by a story and a body, by a larger project that contains it and brings it to life. In Lohana's statements, phrases are not said to please, even if they try to convince us of something. Her statements are not innocent actions, and at the same time, they are full of an irrepressible passion.

Everything that might seem contradictory and confusing about Lohana has an explanation: her project was never about personal advantage, but rather about growing a movement above all else. Lohana didn't need anyone to explain the mechanics of politics to her; she understood them and hacked them on her own. She could stand on the sidewalks of communism while drinking *mate* with Eva Perón, winking at Kirchnerism. And that was fine, it was perfect because despite contradictions, it didn't matter

---

[1] The carnival parades usually have dancing groups dressed up with feathers and shiny clothes, like cabaret artists.

which party got the best story, but rather that a right had been won and a travesti had been protected from violence, hunger, and oblivion. Pragmatism, you might say... Lohana was to Argentine politics what Bill Belichick was to football: defensive strategy, which includes adapting schemes to take advantage of the other team even forcing turnovers. And that's the point, because there's no sense in playing stylish when your opponent lifts the trophy. Lohana's clarity is what makes us miss her so much. In a world where speeches and narratives are more valuable, she chose the material practices.

Lohana was always very clear about at least three things that we should consider central to her theory: 1) the struggle must be with everyone, from an intersectional perspective; 2) identity serves as a platform for organization, but feminisms need to redefine those limits in order to build a perspective beyond identity; and 3) violence, discrimination, and hatred are not just discourse, they are inscribed on the flesh, and to truly win, we must politicize our bodies. These three lines formed the backbone of many of Lohana's proposals and opened new perspectives in the ways of doing politics. Recovering them is the best way to pay tribute to the greatest Latin American travesti leader. Although it has only been a few years since her passing, in travesti years that is an eternity, and sometimes it even seems that her figure is fading, giving way to new ways of thinking about trans experiences that lose their pathway and flounder in mere narrative.

*Making Collectively*

One of Lohana's key activist skills was understanding the centrality of alliances in producing more effective conquest.

She was the first to present and dispute the idea that travestis embodied much more than a type of disobedient sexual identity; they were also part of the many marginalized groups in post-dictatorial Argentina. The research carried out in *Cumbia, copeteo y lágrimas* (Hiller et al. 2007)[Cumbia, Guzzling, and Tears] and *La gesta del nombre propio* (Berkins and Fernández 2005) [The Feat of One's Own Name] sought to investigate and present to cis readers the multiple oppressions to which travestis were subjected: not only were they denied their identity and the right to express themselves as they wished, but they also received little schooling, were deprived of formal employment, expelled from the health system, and abused in their families. This lack of rights reduced the life expectancy of travestis to well below the standards of even the most impoverished sectors of society. This made it clear that the solution was not simply to call for the end to violence against their identities, but that comprehensive policies were needed.

This is how alliances were built with feminists, academics, political circles, and any organization that could help ensure that trans women were included in the democracy. Above all, they wanted to be taken into account in political life. *"The system has always excluded us, and we don't want to be included just for the sake of sensationalism on talk shows. We want to enter the system. Allowing people to vote for a travesti would be the healthiest thing that could happen to this rarefied politics,"* said Lohana, asking that her life and that of her fellows be taken into account as agents of change and transformation. *"We travestis are the ones who are going to provide the party supplies, the show, the fun, right? We also produce knowledge; we can develop theory,"* said Lohana, calling on feminists to stop seeing travestis as a problem to be solved with policies on sexuality. The solution came hand in hand with social transformation, and that transformation had to be a joint effort. That is why Berkins threw herself into the abortion debate when it was not strictly a cause that concerned her, and she joined forces with the Mothers of Plaza de Mayo when she understood that the trans issue was not just a matter of sexual rights, but a cause for human rights.

She didn't care about measuring oppression. Whether so-and-so had suffered more, or whether they were more or less accepted within the system: the point was to unify all those violations and build a shared discourse from the margins. Even a discourse that goes beyond identity as a unit of analysis and sets out to consider all forms of disobedience that lead to exclusion from social life. "*Self-victimization was the strategy for being accepted*" in Argentine political life, but once inside, Lohana set out to discuss many other issues and fight for much more than her right to be a travesti. She understood that in addition to being a travesti, she was also a migrant, a racialized person, a worker, a victim of violence, a rioter. An identity with layers, like an onion.

*The Problem Is with the Potato*

In 2014, Lohana visited Salta, her hometown, and opened her presentation at the College of Psychologists with this anecdote:

> "*A well-known psychologist, whom I won't name, once asked me why there were so many travestis in Salta. And I replied, tired of those kinds of silly questions: the problem is that empanadas have potatoes here, and potatoes are the*

*problem. The truth is, instead of seeing what I was getting at, she wanted to know why it was happening in Salta... a scientific answer: Look, the problem is the empanada, the empanada has potatoes, and the potatoes are the problem, so we would have to study the empanada... give me a break!"*

Behind that hilarious joke lay something very serious, something Lohana never stopped thinking about: how useful were debates about identity? Was identity an issue exclusive to travestis and trans people? Berkins definitely knew that the right to identity was central, which is why she promoted the creation of the Gender Identity Front, which would achieve the approbation of one of the most important laws in Argentine history and the most notable precedent in the world on the path toward respect for autonomy and the depathologization of trans identities. But in her infinite street smarts, Lohana knew that this was only a point of departure. Identity was the gateway to citizenship, but inhabiting it required deeper debates and actions. Lohana did not understand citizenship as an act of state recognition, but as a furtive practice, made up of small everyday actions. That question from the mysterious psychologist encapsulates much of what we as travestis are tired of hearing, the question about our identity as a great unknown, as if it were something we should have to explain, when cis people are not questioned because they remain supported by their biology.

The travesti identity provided us with a platform to speak out about what we needed to say, but over time it became a tight frame that limited and standardized our discourse. Lohana was interested in breaking down that barrier, presenting herself to society as a travesti who could think beyond these roles socially assigned to travestis. She worked to remove travestis from the entertainment and crime pages of newspapers and allow us to talk and think about economics, politics, ecology, and whatever else we wanted. This commitment by the Argentine trans movement to understand transvestism as a political identity is distinctive in the region and allows us to appreciate in travestis the *"critical value of our differences"* without getting caught up in an essentialist and pathologizing discourse.

Today we cannot stop to explain our identity to radicalized trans-exclusionary feminists and new conservative organizations; there is no time to re-discuss the rights we have won. There is no room to think about feminism that does not include all of us who have been oppressed by the patriarchal system. From the neighborhood queer to the middle-class gay, from the butch dyke to the most femme, from the closeted trans man to the one who decides to perform masculinity with breasts, from the clandestine crossdressers to the silicone-enhanced travesti sex workers. Who is going to dare to police identities? Who is going to tell us how we should name ourselves and what we can or cannot do to our bodies? Those who come with that plan should go check the empanadas and find the trans issue there, because we are busy winning rights.

*My Body as an Inalienable Right*

*"I don't want the right to property or the right to vote if I can't keep my body as an inalienable right,"* Berkins repeats on more than one occasion. This phrase brings us back to one of the central topics of Lohana 's travesti theory: the centrality of the body. In queer theory, performance is the new god; gender is a narrative that becomes real through repetition.

However, queer theory does a poor job of addressing the manifestations of these discourses, the surgeries, techniques, and interventions used to create desirable bodies. About the violence used to produce bodies consistent with a binary representation of sexuality. About the encapsulated breasts of travestis, about their swollen legs as a result of clandestine silicone injections, about those who have been dismembered and raped, about those who have been killed. And Lohana never left behind the bodily experience of her time on the street, at the hands of aggressive clients, at the hands of police violence. For Lohana, the body was the territory where battles were fought, and so politicizing it was urgent in order to win the war.

Return to the body was also a way of escaping the discursivity of feminism, sometimes more concerned with producing floating signifiers than inhabiting them. Reclaiming the territory of practices and thinking about policies that truly transform lives. That is why the obvious steps on which to continue the struggle were access to health and work, because these are what guarantee survival. Words and theories can fill hundreds of pages, but they cannot fill the hungry stomach of the adult travesti who can no longer earn even fifty pesos working the streets. Nine thousand new documents can be issued to travestis and trans people, but if there is a single person who, because their identity is denied, is left without access to a job or housing, everything is wrong. And in that sense, Lohana also gave us a horizon, taking care to put her body on the line and to give substance to what often remains mere ramblings.

Her body was always there, fighting battles, engaging in discussions. Lohana didn't stand at the door asking anyone for permission: she went in and put her chest out to take the blows, and that's something we must also learn in this world of virtuality and social media activism. Sometimes bodies have much more to say than pretty posts and slogans on Instagram and Twitter.

* * *

Lohana left us on February 5, 2016. With her passing, our lives lost a little of their sparkle. That day, no one could help but be overcome with grief. Her last letter fills the void and leaves us with the task of resisting:

> *"Dear friends, my health is very critical and does not allow me to meet with you in person. We have achieved many victories over the years. Now is the time to resist, to fight for their continuity. The time for revolution is now, because we will never return to prison. I am convinced that the engine of change is love. The love that was denied to us is our motivation to change the world. All the hits and contempt I suffered are nothing compared to the infinite love that surrounds me at this moment. Travesti fury always! A hug. Lohana Berkins."*

This is perhaps the fourth legacy of her theory: always resist. No matter how much the winds seem to bring less hostile climates, one must never fully trust the ground gained. Lohana, with one hand raised, closed her speeches by shouting at the top of her lungs, "They shall not pass." They shall not pass over our conquests, over our theories, over the disobedient ways of looking at and inhabiting this world. With the image of Lohana as an amulet and "they *shall not pass*" as a mantra, we face strange times, journeys ahead, new territories to conquer, and at least my heart is filled with confidence when I hear Berkins and her loud travesti voice promising us to continue the struggle.

# A Brief History of Travesti Fury

Once upon a time there was the Travesti Fury. A time without drag queens, without voguing dance, without so many forced intersections. It was a time when trans women wore out their heels on the streets, getting in and out of cars, storming police stations, fleeing from trouble like sex guerrillas. It was a time when travestis didn't beat around the bush. They put men in their place. It was a time when they taught the new generation history by touring them through red-light districts. A time of blowjobs in the park, of hurried sex, of unbridled drunkenness and cocaine. A time of squatter dwellings, street riots, and Molotov cocktails burning down a legislature. There was a time when trans women obeyed no one but the hunger that gnawed at their stomachs.

Today, that fury looks good on screen. It fills the pages of a novel that all cis allies will buy to decorate their coffee tables. It feeds the narrative of those who feel cool among the hipsters. It is represented as a nostalgic evocation of the undisciplined times that gave birth to the present. Now, those who always have the floor tell us tearfully about the travesti shoah and invite us to kneel before the wall and beat our breasts. That fury has been transformed into victimhood and has lost all its charm, its deformity, its unruly vibes, its incorrectness. That fury is just a slogan to sell T-shirts and tote bags, a cliché at the end of a statement where we politely demand our rights from the state.

But that night, when Lohana Berkins took to the stage in the square after the Gender Identity Law was passed, she said that the day of travesti fury was coming. *"You don't know what's coming,"* she threatened. But far from bringing a new wave of chaos, the law led to a scenario of virtual recognition that gradually undermined the rebellious power of transvestism. Suddenly, statistics began to show that most people who had previously identified as travestis now identified as 'trans women', and that abolitionist discourse was encouraging their peers to stop selling sex to clients and instead sell themselves to capitalism or the state. Social policies began to align themselves behind trans issues, and trans people behind social policies. If in the past the body was injected with silicone to seduce clients, now it is inflated with hormones to fit into transnormativity and the standards with which the state imagines trans people. Little by little, that overflowing impatience, that unbridled rudeness, and the hungry fever that fueled travesti rage became whitewashed, domesticated, performative, well-behaved, and combed. Dressed to the nines, ready for the governmental office and the school.

For several years now, I have noticed in different contexts that trans girls younger than me fit the mold of good behavior. In the hospital, for example, when the doctor comes out and says his arrogant NO because the care is suspended or delayed or there are no medications, the girls get up quietly and go home. Sometimes they don't even look up from their phones and just get up and leave without protesting. Once, a doctor didn't want to give me my medication for a purely bureaucratic reason. I argued with the doctor at the door of the office, and when I had the chance, I went in, sat down, and made it clear that there were only two ways he could get me out of there: by giving me my pills (which are my right, by law) or by calling security to remove me by force. When I left the office with my pills in hand, I still had enough courage to shout in the waiting room: *"Girls, there are pills, and if they don't want to give them to you, you have to complain."* A few weeks later, I ran into one of those little brats who always kept quiet, and she admitted to me that after that scene, the doctor shut up and gave pills to everyone who was waiting. That's just one of the many times I've noticed that us older women get pissed off, but the younger girls stay quiet in real life and then at most post a 'story time' on IG telling how they were mistreated at a hospital.

It is fine for new generations to invent new political languages and for the digital world to be almost as important as the real world today. But I am a Marxist travesti and it is impossible for me to put the virtual, the symbolic, and the discursive before the overwhelming brutality of material reality. This text is therefore about left-wing and radicalized critiques and positions that are sure to be upsetting to those who have been participating in bourgeois political correctness. While writing this text, I was chatting with friends, and the first thing that came up was the romanticization of our movement's political past, which today is circumscribed by other realities and dialogues with other political spaces that previously turned their backs on us. I wouldn't be so sure. I have at least two arguments against this: the first is that there is a large portion of our travesti and trans community (perhaps a minority in large cities, but certainly enormous in non-metropolitan areas) that even today has not obtained any benefits from the state policies that are supposed to be the pillars of our new status as trans citizens; the second is that the current political situation shows us that none of our achievements are as secure as we imagined, and in just a few months, Javier Milei's government is dismantling many of the rights that we thought would never be rolled back. Furthermore, since last year, we have seen clearly that those political allies who once represented our demands now look at us askance for using non-binary pronouns and blaming us for their electoral defeat. If this is not the time to be romantic and recover the critical value of our difference, when is?

However, I do not intend to proselytize in this text, but rather to show the historical evidence of strategies that queers and travestis used to fight in those times when we did not have to ask anyone's permission. This text is an invitation to explore a brief history of travesti fury, so that those born into this new generation may know what it was like in times when the only option was struggle, sexual terrorism, and hustling. These archival images and stories are not here to be a morbid evocation of the past, they are not an aesthetic work to decorate the walls of a museum, they are not the story of a fictionalized past. They are the material vestiges of a history of travesti and trans fighters who slapped patriarchy in the face with arrogance, with the pride of those who know they are threatened. This is the legacy to which our program of political action should pay tribute, rather than to American fictions of ballroom culture and Butler's theory of performativity. This is the only true and authentic trans resistance.

*United Faggots of Argentina*

In November 1958, AHORA magazine reported on the existence of a "strange and indecent organization" made up of faggots[2]. This organization was a kind of mutual aid association whose purpose was to raise money to hold parties and provide assistance to queers detained in the pederast[3] wing of the Villa Devoto prison. This story has been known for years through the testimony of Malva Solis, a travesti who migrated from Chile to Argentina in 1943. Recently, the document that confirms her version was published (Queiroz 2023).

Following an investigation prompted by a complaint from the cathedral's butler, who noticed that one of the collection boxes had been tampered with, the police arrested seven faggots whom the press identified by their respective aliases: Juana de Arco, la Negra Tucumana, la Gallega, Guillermina, Malva Loca, Fanny, and la Vaca Mocha. An eighth person, Tanny, managed to escape. The seven Buenos Aires faggots were charged with theft and criminal association, as they had allegedly stolen more than 100,000 pesos (at the time) from various churches. Far from showing shame, the detainees pose coquettishly for the press and even reveal intimate details of their lesbian rivalries. Juana de Arco and Malva Loca are the leaders of the group and declare that the United Faggots is a lodge of seven loyal friends who promise to always go through life together, even to prison. They also recount the tricks they use to identify the most affluent collection boxes while declaring that part of the money they steal from elegant cathedrals

---

[2] This organization's name in Spanish was *Maricas Unidas de Argentina*. The term "marica" was used as a slur against gay people. Today, however, it is used as a political statement against normalization and in support of queer identity. I chose the word "faggot" to translate it, mostly because the term retains the slur's origin and references Larry Mitchell's book *The Faggots & 'Their Friends Between Revolutions.'*

[3] The police used the term "pederast" to describe homosexual people, but it never implied sex with underage boys.

will be donated to the collection boxes of other poor churches. Thus, imitating Robin Hood, these queers commit crimes in the name of the good of their community and the poor.

In her previous statements, Malva Solís presents United Faggots as the first form of political/social organization for travestis and queers in Argentina. The constant arrests suffered during the Perón era and the military dictatorship of 1955  forced queers to think of ways to help each other, especially among those detained in the Devoto Prison. Detentions usually lasted up to 90 days, which meant that many lost their jobs, belongings, and homes, so while some remained in detention, others tried to gather the means to help them. With this form of support, Faggots United was organized to raise money to bring care packages to those detained. According to Malva's statements, they published a rudimentary newsletter with news, gossip, and dates of celebrations, which, when it fell into the hands of the police, triggered a large raid that dismantled the organization.

*Pamela Perez, Vedette*

Between April and May 1963, the show *La Nouvelle Eve* [The new Eve] was presented at the Gran Rex Theater by a group of French artists from the famous *Carrousel* Cabaret from Paris. A year earlier, the famous French transsexual artist Jaqueline Dufresnoy, better known as Coccinelle, had shocked the Buenos Aires public. Coccinelle's visit thrilled spectators who, for the first time, witnessed the technological marvel of a transsexual woman whose body had been surgically altered to turn her into an icon of the new era. Still under the shadow of military governments, the luxury and extravagance of vaudeville shows filled the marquees of Corrientes Avenue. Transformist artists, transsexuals, and travestis were a classic of the genre. So when *La Nouvelle Eve* landed on the shores of the River Plate, the press was desperate to find the new Coccinelle and delved into the intimacies of the show until the secret was revealed. Thus, through gossip and inquiries, they discovered that the famous Pamela Perez, one of the main artists, had previously been a 'man.'

Various notes from the time show the ridicule Pamela was subjected to by journalists who harassed her every night, hoping to get her to make a statement. Faced with indiscreet questions about her sexuality, Pamela stammered awkward murmurs in French and only demanded in perfect Spanish that she would not give a statement unless she was paid. Pamela, of Moroccan-Spanish origin, born in Algeria and based in France, had begun her career as a dancer in several cabaret companies and appeared at the *Carrousel du Paris*, now transformed into a woman, for a modeling audition. She entered Argentina using documentation that listed her previous gender and name, which is why the press quickly alerted the public to this strange Eve.

The controversy surrounding Pamela sparked statements and speculation from her castmates, theater staff, and even René Bardy, the company's director, who assured that although she was listed with a male name, this was due to an error, Even his own wife had checked Pamela's private parts to certify her correct sex. Faced with unbearable harassment from journalists who infiltrated dressing rooms, pursued Pamela in private moments, and harassed the cast, Pamela finally exploded and finished the scandal. One night after the show, she found a journalist in her dressing room who insisted on asking her various questions about her past and her sexuality. At first, Pamela remained silent, but she ended up hitting the journalist to get him out of the dressing room and, once at the theater door, she threw a shoe at him. Photographers captured her visibly upset and barefoot after throwing the shoe, as she walked away from the press shouting, "Bastards! Bastards!"

*Deborah Singer: Stripping Society Bare*

Deborah Singer is one of the key figures in the travesti world since the return to democracy. Since her first appearance in the press in 1983, she has used her dual status as an artist and a sex worker to influence society's thinking about travestis. In her interviews, she openly revealed the most intimate details of her life, such as the first time she was admitted to a Mental Hospital at the age of 17. "*It was because of a very heated argument I had with my mother. Thinking that she wasn't going to give me any more money, I tried to commit suicide by taking pills and cutting my veins. My depression was truly terrible, and they decided to admit me. They kept me there for eight months. I will never forget all that,*" she said when she was still a novice actress and dreamed of "*being a good artist, being famous, and that people like me would be accepted and that people would understand that we are very normal and that we have feelings like any other human being.*"

From her first appearances to her last, Deborah took advantage of the press's morbid curiosity to get her message across. Near the end of her time at Eroticón magazine, she posed completely naked, exposing her genitals on the sole condition that she could also expose "the hypocrisy of a society that marginalizes and condemns her." Along with the photos where Deborah proudly shows her nakedness, she dares to challenge heterosexuals' certainties. When the journalist grumbles because he finds it difficult to understand why travestis do not have genital surgery, Deborah replies: "It's *very complicated for you, who are heterosexual, a boring guy, and who will surely die having only tried pussy.*" About the clients that frequents her at Pan-American Highway, Deborah states that "95% *come to get fucked, to get their asses broken, to be ridden like mares. Some ask for all kinds of things! There are more perverts than you can imagine!*" Doctors, bank managers, judges' secretaries, and politicians were Deborah's regular clients, and she could earn up to $300 a night on the Pan-American Highway.

Irreverent, bawdy, dirty, Deborah's travesti interviews go from sex to politics and from politics to sex nonstop. Each of her public statements fearlessly navigates between the indiscretions of her life as a sex worker and her role as one of the visible leaders of the travesti demand for the right to work on the Pan-American Highway and in cabaret venues. Without fear, Singer's karate-like tongue tells you about the times she had to sleep with guys for a piece of bread, the miseries she experienced with her friends, and the times voyeurs and perverts paid her exotic fortunes for the most indecent carnal acts.

*Karina Urbina's Edgy Transsexuality*

Trans disobedience is not just about making heterosexuals uncomfortable. Karina Urbina embodied a key aspect of the transsexual struggle that brought a completely new perspective to the civil rights struggle of the 1990s. During her traditional Wednesday protests at various government agencies, Karina Urbina's solitary struggle for legal recognition of sex change[4] and the amendment of Article 91 of the Penal Code shaped a universe of demands that was almost fifteen years ahead of its time. When no travesti was concerned about issues of identity, health, education, or work, Karina Urbina had a clear political platform where legal recognition of sex was the gateway to a dignified life. Karina Urbina's ideas were unpleasant for the movement of her time. The media's exposure, the spectacularization of politics during the Menem era, and the centrality of visibility policies were not friendly terrain for the ideas of a woman who only wanted to be recognized as such in order to have a peaceful life and disappear from the public scrutiny.

Between 1991 and 1996, her activism strongly supported gay and lesbian spaces, and she became the first trans person in the organization of the First Pride Parade in Buenos Aires, but over time, alliances with travestis to fight against misdemeanor codes pushed Karina's demands into the background. *"Time will show who the real activists are,"* (Urbina 19996) she said in one of her last letters. And time certainly proved her right. Once the debate over misdemeanor codes was over, the travesti movement faced a new political landscape that, although it never recognized Karina Urbina's central role, took up her slogans and strategies and transformed them under the queer perspective on gender and feminism. Thus, the fight for the Gender Identity Law owes much of its previous jurisprudence, legal efforts, and political debates to the transsexual activism of Karina Urbina and others who, concerned with being recognized as women, opened the

---

[4] I use the term 'sex change' because it better represents the ideas circulating in the second half of the 21st century. Today trans people use 'gender affirmation surgeries' to name these medical practices.

door for everyone to be recognized in their chosen gender.

## Travesti Scandals

The 1990s were the epicenter of the biggest travesti scandals. More than once, police stations, the Buenos Aires legislature, and other public buildings were vandalized and even set on fire as part of travesti protests. On July 2, 1998, a particularly striking and radical riot took place that symbolized the enormous power of the travesti activism led at that time by Lohana Berkins and Nadia Echazú. After police refused to allow travestis to enter the legislative chamber where a substantial amendment to the City of Buenos Aires Urban Coexistence Code was being discussed, a group of about 50 travestis began a protest. The police officers decided that they would only allow people with IDs to enter, which enraged the travestis gathered on the steps of the legislative palace. The measure, clearly taken to hinder the participation of travestis in the session, sparked an unexpected reaction: the travestis, led by Lohana Berkins, began to tear up their ID cards in front of the stunned guards. "*I am not just a document, I am Jessica,*" one of them said, while others showed that their ID cards did not have a single stamp in the electoral section, proving that they had always been excluded from democracy. Lohana herself tore up her ID card while saying, "*Comrades, those of you who have ID cards, take them out! We are going to tear them up so they can see what we do with those documents.*" "*The ID cards were never useful to us,*" shouted one, "*Show them the photo,*" said another. "*There you have the ID's, this is a farce, they don't respect us even with these IDs, now they want to demand IDs*". The legislature has to recognize that it has lost the battle with the Federal Police," Lohana declares before the TV cameras, while an up in arms Nadia shouts, "We're not leaving Palermo, they're going to kill us in Palermo, but we're not leaving. We are citizens, we are neighbors of Palermo, we pay taxes, and we have the right to walk around here."(Archivo Prisma 2023)

This example, but also many other travesti scandals led by Lohana and Nadia fueled travesti rage. In 1999, a sit-in outside the legislature ended in repression between travestis and the police. Several times, police stations were broken into, patrol cars were destroyed, and the travestis managed to make the police look ridiculous. Also in 1999, a picket line outside the UK embassy during a visit from the Prince of Wales, to whom the travestis were requesting political asylum, ended in a huge scandal. In 2003, the legislature was set on fire by a group of travestis and street vendors who opposed new amendments to the Urban Coexistence Code during Macri's administration in the city. The mix of travestis and picketers was at the forefront of the struggles of the early 21st century, and figures such as Diana Sacayan and Maité Amaya embodied the struggle of the working classes side by side with 'sexual minorities.'

The scandal among travestis has a distinct and particular value. It is a momentary seizure of power, which allows the equation to be reversed for a few seconds, placing the power to hurt in the hands of the travestis. In Scandalous Acts, Don Kulick and Charles Klein discuss the politics of shame, analyzing how travestis, through scandal, have the power to shame clients and, in doing so, renegotiate rates, conditions, and violence. Scandal draws attention to the travestis' denunciation, to their complaint in the face of an unjust situation, forcing the aggressors to look down with shame and to hide from the possible revenge of their rage (Kulick and Klein 2009). The scandal allows the travesti to flee the scene and take refuge. Making a scandal makes them a notorious subject and thus humanizes them. Therefore, far from being a hysterical and exaggerated attitude, making a scandal is one of the many forms of survival that travestis have invented to force pimps to feel ashamed. Just as nudity in a theatrical scene breaks with the convention of the fourth wall and returns the viewer to their place as a voyeur; for travestis, scandal and nudity force others to look away, afraid of being discovered in their desire.

*Inhabiting Perverse Citizenship*

Of course, my view of these past events is tinged with romanticism. I confess to being unconditionally in love with history. The political key to the present does not (yet) seem to enable scandal, crime, violence, and nudity as a key to political agency. However, these evocations of the past are a good invitation to think about what kind of trans citizenship we want to build for future generations. Marcia Ochoa describes a type of trans citizenship that she calls 'perverse citizenship.' Ochoa says: "*There are many trans women who are or want to be good citizens, but I think it is important that our political vision is not limited by the expectation that we will all want to be good citizens. An 'ungrateful' person is similar to Sara Ahmed's figure of the 'feminist killjoy'; she is someone who breaks the heteropatriarchal social contract. Someone who can't go along with the joke because they don't find it funny. (…) Unlike a persona non grata or an unwelcome citizen—who are effectively formally rejected by the state—an ungrateful person rejects society and the state on their own behalf. They are ungrateful, resentful. Trans women have every reason in the world to be resentful and ungrateful to society—the miracle for me is that not all of them are."* (Ochoa 2008) Thus, Ochoa advocates for a non-normative citizenship, that is, a type of citizenship that does not force us to adapt and behave, but rather incorporates dissent, whoring, and bad vibes.

Based on these insights into scandal and ingratitude, and with this evidence of a not-so-distant past, I want us to think about how we will, especially in this context of the almost total defeat of progressivism, feminism, and the LGBT agenda, create a new political horizon. A new horizon that is not a lethargic celebration of institutional achievements, that is not a tribute to the rainbow flag, a bureaucratic and formal parade down the sidewalk covered in glitter. That's it, girls. The time for asking the state for things, for celebrating 'the first trans person to accomplish something' is over. What good is it to have so many first trans people if there is no room for others after them? How much longer are we going to celebrate the creation of a LGBT office, the lighting up of the city's monument with rainbow colors, and the election of a trans queen pageant winner in an agricultural festival? This is getting out of hand.

We must demand much more: we must question privileges, no matter how small, and deal with dissent, chaos, and shouting in assemblies. If we want to preserve some of that explosive power of travesti fury, we have to accept that there are comrades who don't want to be white, skinny, pretty, non-binary, on hormones, long-haired, short-haired, busty, or flat-chested. We have to love ourselves with our monstrosity, with our political nonconformity, and with our radicalism. Only then will we have a chance to fight on all possible fronts: there will be those who want to be the ministerial official in a tailored suit, those who, like me, want to fight within the academic world, those who want to dance ballroom, those who recite poetry, those who suck a cop's dick and steal his wallet, those who create a cooperative, and those who write tweets. But we have to build a political program with all of them, even if we are often ashamed. The important thing is that we do not allow ourselves to be consumed by hegemonic discourses on political conscience. We have always had our own ways of fighting, and we have built them in opposition to the morality of the Argentine bourgeoisie. The politicians will continue to form their parties, fighting their internal disputes, fighting with the Trotskyists, playing at being trolls on the Internet; but our veins are filled with hunger and we cannot (and besides, we are not invited anyway) to play bourgeois politics. We have inherited travesti fury and we have a historical duty to use our dirty and forbidden desires to build politics that makes it possible for a generation to survive us and continue to fight from the critical value of our difference.

# History of Travesti Trans Activism in Argentina: Political Itineraries in Tension

Writing about the history of political processes is always challenging. It is a subject as alive as flesh and blood, involving partisan disputes, legacies, and futures. I will nevertheless take the risk to review in this text the political activities of Argentine travestis, trans, and transsexual people from the second half of the 20th century to the present. The aim is not to set in stone an official history of trans people in Argentina, but rather to produce some basic historical guidelines to organize political and historiographical debates. For this purpose, I will use the notion of political itineraries[5], introduced by Lohana Berkins in *Un Itinerario Político del Travestismo* (Berkins 2008) [A Political Itinerary of Transvestism]. We might consider this text as the foundation work on the historical concern with trans issues in Argentina. Berkins constructs a chronology that shows the formation of the first organizations and spaces for political action, the formation of coalitions with feminists and human rights organizations, and the significant events of a struggle agenda between 1991 to 2003. But this chronological order proposed by Berkins is only one of many possible itineraries. Each itinerary reflects a narrative voice and focuses on a particular type of experience. Therefore, in order to produce a history of travesti/trans activism in Argentina, we must

---

[5] I decided to translate Berkins's term 'itinerarios políticos' literally as 'political itineraries,' trying to maintain the ambiguity of the term "itinerary," which is usually used to describe a journey or travel plan. In this case, however, it is used to describe the trajectories and agendas of the travesti activist movement.

collect and systematize these itineraries and confront their tensions and contradictions.

There is another political itinerary strongly popular among younger generations and encompasses the legislative achievements of the last decade, from the enactment of the Gender Identity Law in 2012 to the present. This 'post-Berkins' itinerary focuses on the demands that travesti and trans organizations made to the Argentine government, which were channeled into legislative initiatives and the creation of spaces within the government from which to promote specific actions for the trans population. It is an itinerary centered on public policies that has been vigorously supported by LGBT organizations, travesti and trans associations, and political parties identified with the progressist wing of Peronism. Although this narrative is recognized as the legacy to the struggles of leaders such as Lohana Berkins and Diana Sacayan, it does not delve into the complex tensions between grassroots activism and state initiatives. Finally, there is a third political itinerary still developing, led by the oldest travestis, self-denominated as 'the historical ones' [las históricas], which aims to reconstruct the moments and strategies that preceded formal activism. The most recent is a collection of stories, memories, and audiovisual records produced by travestis who survived the extreme violence perpetrated by the Argentine state between the last military dictatorship (1976-1983) and the return to democracy (1983-1994). This narrative voice highlights the strategies of peer support, cunning in the face of police control, and the first forms of assembly and anarchy that developed under the umbrella of sex work.

Obviously, there are other necessary and urgent political itineraries in Argentina, such as non-metropolitan activism, transmasculine, and non-binary activism, although their development is still limited to a few research projects. In this text, I will focus on the interweaving of all these paths to construct a timeline that arbitrarily encompasses a complex set of travesti, transsexual, and transgender political experiences. I will divide this timeline based on some significant events that allow us to establish temporal milestones and extreme dates.

*United Faggots of Argentina and the First Lawsuits for the Recognition of Transsexual Identity (1951-1986)*

There is a wide variety of sources available to document trans history in Argentina: medical, legal, police, psychiatric, and criminal records, etc., produced by the governments and its agents; editorial archives produced by journalists and photojournalists; memoirs and biographies; other literary and film archives, etc. Memoirs are especially useful for reconstructing certain periods, as they record terms, experiences, and identifications that were censored or omitted in other kinds of records. It is through one of these biographical memoirs, that of Malva Solís, that we can learn about one of the first attempts at political organization in the country: United Faggots of Argentina (UFA).

UFA was a mutual aid group founded in 1951 by gay and queer people detained in Devoto Prison accused of wearing clothes contrary to their gender or offering sex in public. These two actions had been classified as crimes against morality in Buenos Aires police ordinances in 1935. As a result, persecution of queer people was commonplace when Malva Solís moved from Chile to Buenos Aires in the 1940s

(Cutuli and Insausti 2015). Each of these detentions in Devoto could last up to sixty days, during which time they suffered from hunger and cold. That is why they decided to create a support system among queers, where each one contributed some money to help those detained with the promise of being helped in the event of a future arrest. In addition, UFA had a homemade newsletter through which queers learned about the situation of those detained, community news, gossip, and invitations to parties and meetings. On one occasion, one of the copies fell into the hands of the police and triggered a large raid, after which this early attempt at organization was dismantled.

During this period, the word *marica* [faggot] referred to a wide spectrum of sex-gender experiences that cannot be reduced to what we today name as travesti. The word travesti became popular in 1971 after the presentation in Buenos Aires of the group "*Les Girls*," a group of Brazilian artists who "dressed up" as women as part of a theatrical performance (Cytryn 2021). The term was used to refer to other artists (always suspected of being effeminate) who cross-dressed. Later, the word travesti was also used to refer to those who wore women's clothing and had undergone silicone and/or hormone treatments and engaged in sex work. Outside of this characterization, another type of gender experience developed: transsexual identity.

In 1966, a very popular newspaper reported on a court case involving 'sex change' surgeries. Doctors Clemente Rodríguez Jáuregui, Alejandro Pavlosky, Ricardo San Martín, and Francisco Defazio were accused for the 'mutilation' of five transsexual patients: Liliana Vega, María Vega, Derito Armesto, Marta Fábregas, and Patricia Rojo.

The controversy began after Maria Vega filed a lawsuit seeking recognition of her identity in her documents, claiming that she had changed her sex through surgery. The courts investigated the doctors, imprisoned them, and finally acquitted them in 1969. This controversy led to the reform of the Medical Practice Acts, to ban surgeries on reproductive organs without prior judicial authorization. This event promoted the political decision of the Argentine government to regulate the bodily self-determination of transsexual people.

*The Travesti's Front and the Pan-American Highway Crimes (1986–1993)*

In the 1980s, some red-light districts began to form around the neighborhoods in northern Buenos Aires, and gradually spread toward the Pan-American Highway. Unlike in previous times, when travestis worked alongside cisgender women and pretending to be cisgender, the Pan-American Highway red-light district was recognized by clients, the police, and neighbors as exclusively for travestis. The performance of travestis, inspired by theater and cabarets, moved to the streets. This decade was also marked by the emergence of clandestinely applied silicone injections, a technology that allowed travestis to build voluptuous figures while avoiding the negative effects of hormone therapy.

Between 1983 and 1993, nearly one hundred travestis were murdered in Pan-American Highway in at least three different ways: crimes directly related to police violence, murders characterized as 'crimes of passion,' and accidental deaths while fleeing between cars. Newspapers speculated that there was a serial killer whom they called 'The butterfly hunter[6].' Fabiola, an 18-year-old Paraguayan travesti, was run over by a patrol car, and her death encouraged her friends to protest. Led by Mónica Ramos and Perica Burrometo, travestis living in Tigre and other neighborhoods in the northern zone of the city protested for the first time on December 21, 1986. They arrived at Plaza de Mayo with banners reading *"We want tolerance,"* *"Stop the abuse," and "We want equal rights,"* while displaying the bruises made by the police and showing their bodies. This group proclaimed itself the Travesti's Front and submitted a list of demands to Interior Minister Antonio Troccoli.

The Travesti's Front aimed to become an union for sex workers, but it was dismantled due to police repression, forcing its leaders into exile or leading to their deaths. This event demonstrates that the violence experienced by travestis during the dictatorship continued and even intensified during the first years of democratic restoration.

*The First Organizations and Debates on Travesti Identity (1993-1997)*

The first trans organization to participate in pride parades and raise awareness of their issues in the media was Transexuals for the Right to Identity and Life. It was founded in 1991 by Karina Urbina, a prominent transsexual activist, editor of Confidencial Magazine, and director of the first trans-themed magazine in Argentina: The Transsexual Voice. The political actions of Urbina and other transsexual women of the 1990s, such as Patricia Gauna, Yanina Moreno, and Mariela Muñoz, constitute a transsexual political trajectory that deserves a specific and detailed study.

---

[6] In Spanish-speaking cultures "mariposa" (butterfly) has historically been a derogatory term for effeminate men.

Carlos Jáuregui and his colleagues from Gays for Civil Rights were interested in including travestis in the parades and other activities, but their reality as young, middle-class gay men had little to do with the marginalized conditions of travestis. Travestis accessed gay and lesbian spaces through two paths: legal assistance provided by Angela Vanni and the Metropolitan Community Church, a congregation led by Pastor Roberto González. These welcoming spaces provided the first opportunities for travestis to organize. In 1993, United Travestis participated in the second Pride Parade. Although it presented itself as an organization founded by Kenny de Michelis, Sandy González, and Gabriela Carrizo, not many people were actually involved in this group. Also in 1993, during a birthday party, a group of travestis noticed the absence of some guests who had been arrested on their way there. Tired of the persecution, Claudia Pía Baudracco, María Belén Correa, Dahiana Diet, Alejandra Romero, Cinthia Pérez, Wendy Leguizamon, Veruska, Fidela Colman, Sara Gómez, and Jeanet Contreras founded the Argentine Travesti Association (ATA).

Two other central figures of travesti activism were prominent on the scene during those years. Lohana Berkins participated in the founding of the Association of Sex Workers of Argentina and was vice president of the Argentine Homosexual Community. In 1994, she witnessed ATA's participation in the third Pride March and approached the group, feeling that she needed to become politically active alongside other travestis. Also in 1994, Nadia Echazú made contact with ATA through an invitation from Angela Vanni. Therefore, from 1994 to 1997, ATA was the space that brought together the main travesti activists, although not without tensions. In 1995, they held two large-scale demonstrations: a sit-in in front of the Casa Rosada under the slogan *"We sit down so we can walk,"* demanding the repeal of police edicts, and organizing the March Against Police Violence, jointly with the University of Buenos Aires, human rights, and LGBT organizations (Fernández Romero 2019).

In 1996, the 1st National Lesbian, Gay, Travesti, Transsexual, Transgender Meeting was held in Rosario. This meeting, spearheaded by Carlos Jáuregui, served as a catalyst for shared concerns and experiences and definitively established the acronym LGBT as a space for political articulation. In 1997, the political tensions between Lohana, Nadia, and the founders of ATA became evident. The focus of the disputes was sex work, while ATA had adopted a neutral position on the issue, Nadia wanted to take a stance in favour of sex work and openly acknowledge her status; and Lohana preferred a more nuanced approach that addressed sex work without explicitly endorsing it. These controversies led to the creation of the Organization of Travestis and Transsexuals of Argentina, founded by Nadia Echazú, and the Association for the Struggle for Travesti and Transsexual Identity, led by Lohana Berkins.

*Lohana Berkins and Coalition Strategies (1997–2012)*

The political strategy that distinguished Lohana Berkins from other travesti activists of her generation was the creation of coalition spaces with feminist groups, academic groups, and human rights organizations. When she founded the Association for the Struggle for Travesti and Transsexual Identity, Lohana already had in mind a universe of original political demands. Her strategy was to move beyond the issue of sex work and the fight against the code of misdemeanors, without abandoning it entirely, to advance the right to identity, understanding it as the gateway to other fundamental rights.

Between 1994 and 1999, the central issue for activists was the repeal of ordinances 2H and 2F, which criminalized offering sex and wearing clothing considered inappropriate for one's assigned sex. With the autonomization of the City of Buenos Aires, following the 1994 constitutional reform, the debate on codes of misdemeanors opened up, in which travesti activists participated to achieve the finishing to police persecution. During those years, the conflict between travesti sex workers and residents of the fanciest neighborhoods occupied the front pages and prime time of the media, and travestis appeared on television to popularize their demands. Lohana differentiated herself from this media strategy and built political alliances in a different way. When the ordinances became ineffective following the enactment of the new urban coexistence code in 1998, Lohana deepened her activism and progressively approached feminist assemblies, academic spaces such as the Sexual Politics Group of the University of Buenos Aires, and the Mothers of Plaza de Mayo. Other fundamental alliances were constituted through left-wing parties, and she was hired in 1999 as an advisor to Congressman Patricio Echegaray of the Communist Party.

Through the Mothers of Plaza de Mayo publishing house in 2005, Lohana Berkins and Josefina Fernández published The Feat for One's Own Name, the first report on the situation of the travesti/trans community in Argentina. In 2007, she published Cumbia, Guzzling, and Tears and participated in El Teje Magazine, an editorial project directed by Marlene

Wayar with the support of the Ricardo Rojas Cultural Center of the University of Buenos Aires. Also in 2007, she spearheaded the creation of the "Nadia Echazú" Textile Co-op, a project for the labor inclusion of travesti and trans people. In 2011, she was involved in the founding of the first high school for trans people, the "Mocha Celis" High School.

This network of alliances was undoubtedly key to Lohana's political trajectory and to the achievement of the Gender Identity Law in 2012. True to her strategy, Lohana promoted the creation of the Front for Gender Identity, a space that brought together gay, travesti, trans, and other allied groups. From this platform, a Gender Identity Law bill was promoted to counter the one presented by the Argentine LGBT Federation. While the LGBT Federation's bill included requirements for stability and permanence in gender identity, the Front's bill promoted the notion of self-perception and advocated for access to trans-specific healthcare as a central and indivisible part of the right to identity. The passage of the Gender Identity Law bill in 2012 crowned Lohana Berkins' political strategy and served as a catalyst for demands for the right to employment, education, and healthcare for the travesti/trans population.

*Gender Identity Law and Trans Labor Quota Law, a Decade of Public Policy (2012–2022)*

The right of accessing ID cards that reflect self-perceived identity also represented access to citizenship for trans and travesti people. This key concept of trans citizenship is the central focus of the last decade of political achievements. The coalitions forged by Lohana Berkins deepened during this period, consolidating the idea that trans rights are human rights and therefore must be addressed by society as a whole. Travesti and trans participation in feminist movements increased, although resistance from conservative sectors persists. Travestis also joined social movements, and labor organizations. Maite Amaya, a travesti activist from Córdoba, participated in the Federation of Grassroots Organizations (FOB), embodying an anarchic and critical voice regarding the patriarchal practices of working-class political organizations and feminist movements. Diana Sacayán founded the Anti-Discrimination Liberation Movement, from which she promoted inclusion projects for the LGBT population in the shantytowns and working-class neighborhoods of the La Matanza district, Buenos Aires Province. Lohana Berkins deepened her participation in the National Campaign for the Right to Legal, Safe, and Free Abortion, extending the debate on abortion to the field of bodily autonomy and the right to self-determination.

Access to work, health, and education were the main issues on the agenda of travesti/trans activism after the approbation of the Gender Identity Law. Lohana Berkins and Diana Sacayán promoted trans employment inclusion projects under the slogan of the "*derecho al travajo*" (right to work, written with a v instead b in reference to the word travesti) In 2015, a law was passed in the Province of Buenos Aires establishing a 1% quota in the public administration. Many universities and federal institutions established similar quotas in their jurisdictions. In the health sector, intense disputes arose over the effective implementation of Article 11 of the Gender Identity Law, which establishes that hormonal and surgical treatments for the personal development of trans people must be guaranteed in the public health system. In 2015, some specific services for trans individuals were established, sometimes referred to as trans-friendly clinics, and the Ministry of Health drafted guidelines and recommendations. Trans and non-binary activist groups, particularly in Buenos Aires, held assemblies to protest the shortages of hormones during the Mauricio Macri administration, and in 2018, they created the Trans Resource Guide, a website that collectively compiles information on healthcare services for trans people.

In 2017, Marlene Wayar presented the *"Reconocer es reparar"* [To Recognize Is to Repair] project, a legislative initiative aimed at obliging the Argentine State to acknowledge its responsibility for the crimes and offenses committed against travesti and trans people during the military dictatorship and the subsequent democratic period. Drawing on the concept of genocide, Marlene proposed the notion of 'travesticide' as a particular form of state-sponsored extermination focuses on dissident sexual identities. In 2012 and 2014, Buenos Aires legislator Maria Rachid had presented similar projects, which were met with rejection from society and the media. In line with the demands for historical reparations, the Trans Memory Archive was founded in 2014.

The social agitation surrounding the debate on the right to abortion in 2018 brought the issue of who has abortions into public discussion, demonstrating that cisgender women are not the only ones who have abortions. Organizations such as *Putos Mal* [bad faggots] and the Transmasculine Front intervened in the debates, demanding that the right to abortion include trans men. Lesbians and Feminists for the Decriminalization of Abortion also intervened to challenge the notion of women as the sole gestating body. These debates provided the foundation for the deepening of transmasculine and non-binary activism. Eugenio Talbot Wright, Blas Radi, Mauro Cabral, and other activists established theoretical and programmatic bases for contemporary transmasculine activism.

In 2020, the Ministry of Women, Gender and Diversity was created within the national government, and Presidential Decree No. 721/2020 was enacted, establishing a 1% trans employment quota in the national public administration. On June 24, 2021, the legislative chambers approved Law No. 27.636 on Access to Formal Employment for Travesti, Transsexual, and Transgender People, named "Diana Sacayán-Lohana Berkins." Also in 2021, a third category for recording sex was established through a presidential decree, indicated by the letter X. This enables gender to be registered in a non-binary way.

We still need more theoretical and methodological debates about perspectives on trans history in the region. This essay is a first attempt to bring together a complex set of political experiences on a single timeline. However, many parts of the narrative remain open, requiring further development and in-depth exploration in future research. It is the task of the new generation of researchers and social scientists to translate memory into history, with all the responsibilities that this mission entails. After so many years of being narrated from outside the trans community, the time has come to reclaim the narrative of history and recover the power of a vast universe of practices, experiences, and emotions that still remain submerged beneath the waters of academic cissexism.

# Peace, Land, and Bread: Travesti Memories for Thinking and Working the Streets

The first thirty travestis who demonstrated on December 21, 1986, in front of the Casa Rosada were not ashamed of being sex workers. When they organized to protest, they were clear that what mattered most to them was that they be allowed to work in peace and that the killings stop. That first protest was fueled by their anger from having lost fifteen colleagues in a few months and the certainty that the police would continue to persecute them every night. To carry out their demands, they chose the political language and strategies characteristic of their time. Mónica Ramos, for example, organized the Travesti's Front with the girls from the neighborhoods surrounding the Pan-American Highway. This was the first documented example of travesti organization and was responsible for the demonstrations on December 21 and 28, 1986, in front of the Casa Rosada. Later, the leaders and members of the front were the focus of media attention, which reported on the political program of this space of struggle.

In an interview with the magazine Libre on August 27, 1987, Mónica Ramos detailed the main concerns of the travestis who work on Pan-AmericanHighway:

> I'm tired of all of us always having to live hiding in the dark because we can't work freely. We've been beaten, threatened, and nobody cares. Does anyone care that fifteen of us have already died on the Pan-American Highway? Of

*course, they forget that those who died are human beings, regardless of whether they work as travestis. Look, I've been working on the street for seventeen years and I've always done so freely, but now I don't know why they're persecuting us. That's why I'm fighting alongside my folks, and if they've chosen me to defend them, I'll do it even if it costs me my life.*

Monica and her friends considered that offering sex was a legitimate job, perhaps the only job available to them due to the discrimination they suffered in society. They certainly did not refer to their lifestyle as sexual exploitation. For this reason, the Travesti's Front sought to align itself with the workers' struggles, as they understood that they were doing legitimate work and should be covered by the same legal protections.

In the same interview, Mónica mentioned the protests held in Plaza de Mayo in December 1986, when they delivered a letter addressed to President Raúl Alfonsín. They never received a response to that letter. Mónica therefore recounts what decisions were made afterwards to further their struggle:

*Because of the persecution we face, they are afraid to go to work on the Pan-American Highway; but if we don't do it, no one knows that we are starving, because each of the girls has to pay rent, eat, and buy clothes. Because of all our suffering, we are sending letters inside and outside the country inviting all travestis to join in a union, since we have no one to protect us. We plan to go see Ubaldini at the CGT (the main worker union in Argentina) to ask him if they will defend us against any problems we may have once we become a union. And we'll fight to achieve this.*

The Travesti's Front undoubtedly had more aspirations than real possibilities of materialization. The urgent need for the travestis to fill their stomachs and solve their daily life problems had priority over any possibility of planning for the future. Police pressure and constant mass raids also undermined the political struggle carried out by the travestis, although without extinguishing it completely. A small newspaper clipping from Diario Crónica recounts how, during a police operation in which *"twenty-four tigresses with stilettos and claws"* were arrested, some travestis who managed to escape by bus and shouted from the windows with their fists raised, *"Alfonsín, we want freedom!"* and *"No to repression!"* However, constant threats and arrests intimidated the travestis, and even Mónica Ramos had to take refuge in Montevideo, Uruguay, for a long time. When she returned to Argentina in 1990, she spent just four months visiting friends and trying to reorganize the Front, but then she was brutally murdered on the Pan-American Highway.

## Memory Is a Red-Light District

This article will address the issue of sex work from a travesti perspective, attempting to move beyond the debate between sex work defenders and sex work abolitionism that has become entrenched in the feminist agenda. I am interested in considering the experience of offering sex as a space for encounter, debate, organization, and meaning-making for travestis, beyond the political controversies that currently permeate this field of debates. With this in mind, I will draw on documentary work focused on recovering the voices of travestis who participated in the early years of organization and struggle. I will attempt to highlight those life trajectories that, although of central importance to the collective history of travestis, are not yet widely known. The explanation for this lack of visibility of the memories of travestis in relation to the experience of the sex work deserves a thorough analysis of how the political agendas of trans movements were drawn up during the first decades of the 21st century in alliance with feminism, human rights movements, and LGBT organizations.

The memory of the trans movement is a subject of constant turmoil and a field of repeated disputes. Sometimes, it functions as a red-light district where everyone is disputing the best spot. Over the last decade, and especially since the enactment of the Gender Identity Law, there have been various narrative efforts to construct a genealogy of the struggle of trans and non-binary people. Understanding how different fields of political action have been formed, the centrality of certain events, and the impact of some fundamental achievements allows us to redefine strategies and modes of intervention and coordination between civil society organizations and the government. Narrating a history of the trans community that fits society's political agendas ultimately enables political intervention to achieve future goals.

In this scenario, archives become an attractive arena in which to resolve disputes and express tensions. Building a memory for certain social movements requires producing excerpts that bring light on certain events and leaders, while obscuring other trajectories. This is why investigating a community's memory not only allows us to understand the historical processes that constitute it, but also to access the current discourses that politicize these narratives. We therefore understand that remembering is not disconnected from current political, social, and cultural processes; rather, the past and present are intertwined in the production of memories.

That is why in this article I propose to investigate how the current disputes between sectors in favor of and against the sex work have strained the way in which travesti and trans community produces its memories. The street, the offer of sex, and the violence associated with it can be interpreted from different perspectives, but only those that become socially necessary to produce languages of demand within organizations and before government agencies are privileged and institutionalized.

*Political Repertoires for Thinking and Working on the Streets*

As we saw in the previous story about the organizational experience of the Travesti's Front, the political language of workers' demands proved useful in a historical period of intense labor riots. The return to democratic life was accompanied by a rebirth of union activity, expressed in numerous demonstrations and general strikes against the economic policies of the Alfonsín government. Although journalists highlight this in a quasi-jocular tone, comparing Mónica to Ubaldini, this key to political action made sense for the canon of democracy in the 1980s. A similar story marked the birth of the Argentine Travestis Association (ATA) in 1993. María Belén Correa recounts that founding moment:

> We had to have a name. The first word was union: Travestis'
> Union. But because there were girls who weren't sex
> workers, they said no, because they wouldn't be associated

*with sex work. For example, Wendy, who was a teacher but worked in a nightclub in the cloakroom; Cinthya, who worked as a nurse; and there were two or three others who didn't want the union theme. There were also some who couldn't be visible because of their family situation, because they could be kicked out of their rented accommodation. I don't remember if it was Pía or Alejandra who said, "Why don't we use the name the police officer gave us?" Ten days ago, when we were trying to get into the apartment with Alejandra and Pía, a police officer came to arrest us. So we started saying no, that "I live here, I'm entering my apartment, here's the key, I'm wearing pants." We started arguing and the police officer said to us, "But who are you? Are you from the Argentine travestis' association?" And they took us away... (Aversa and Máximo 2021)*

The idea of a union for this new period was problematic because it meant link political action exclusively to the issue of sex work. As María Belén points out, not all the girls were involved in sex work or could formally acknowledge it, but they understood the need for an organization. Although they avoided framing their activism around the issue of sex work, the early years of the travestis' struggle in the 1990s were marked by this concern. Misdemeanor codes were in full force, and police persecution of travestis in the city of Buenos Aires was as intense as or even more intense than in the days of Pan-American Highway.

During these years, travestis began to articulate their demands alongside gay and lesbian movements. Both groups shared a common concern about police persecution. Gays and lesbians were repeatedly detained during police raids on nightclubs or while walking in cruising areas. This shared problem of the right to move freely in public spaces served to unify the demands of gays, lesbians, and travestis. Under the paradigm of associativism and non-governmental organizations, gays, lesbians, and travestis developed a new language of demand focused on the fight against misdemeanor codes. The focus shifted partially from the issue of sex work to free movement in public spaces.

It is worth mentioning, however, that gay activists at that time had the vocation and strategy of centralizing and bringing together different individuals affected by the issue of sexual persecution in Argentina, beyond any ideological and/or moral debate. The members of Gays for Civil Rights (GCR) were constantly on the lookout for activist initiatives that could align with their struggles, which is how they took the initiative to integrate travestis. First, they made contact with United Travestis, a small organization founded by Kenny de Michelis, Sandy Gonzalez, and Gabriela Carrizo. GCR sponsored their public presentations and made them part of their meetings. United Travestis accompanied the Second Pride Parade in 1993. That year, GCR contacted ATA, inviting them to participate in meetings. During these meetings, the members of ATA got in touch with Angela Vanni, the GCR's lawyer, who worked tirelessly with the travestis every time they were arrested. She defended them in many of the cases that the police arbitrarily brought forward, using planted evidence as a way to intimidate and deactivate the most high-profile activists (Ferreyra 2020).

During these meetings with Angela Vanni, a core group of travesti activists concerned about the incessant arrests began to form. All or most of them were involved in the sex work, although they had different opinions on the matter. In 1994, Nadia Echazú, who had been put in touch with Angela Vanni through Kenny de Michelis, recounted the following:

> Angela arranged for me to meet with United Travestis (UT) one day, but I didn't like their approach and I could see that what they were doing didn't translate to the rest of the girls. The police didn't bother them, but they also didn't do anything to prevent the girl next to them from being taken away. Angela noticed this and invited me to a meeting with Belén [Correa] from ATA. We started working together.

Some time later, Lohana Berkins also joined those meetings with Ángela through her connection with Carlos Jáuregui. Lohana says:

> I had left the Argentine Homosexual Community, where I had been secretary, and I met ATA at that pride parade, where they participated for the first time. I went there, but as a member of the Argentine Sex Workers Association, because I was one of the founders (...) And that's where we met, and I told myself that I had to get more involved with the trans women, so one day I called Ángela and she took me to an ATA meeting, and I stayed there.

Between 1994 and 1996, this space brought together the leading travesti activists of the time: Lohana Berkins, Nadia Echazú, Claudia Pía Baudracco, and Maria Belen Correa. The debates and working groups between these activists, grouped together in ATA, were not without tension. Often, this conflict had to do with the issue of sex work, which constantly emerged as a key factor. In an interview conducted by Ana Álvarez and Josefina Fernández in 2001,

Lohana retrospectively discussed the differences that existed in that space in a dialogue with Nadia Echazú:

> *You have to remember this, because you had a very interesting stance. When we discussed the issue of prostitution and argued about it in meetings. You supported prostitution, bluntly. And I supported prostitution, but I asked the question "why?" There was a question… Why are we prostitutes? And Belén said we had to talk about AIDS. But even with our differences, there was consistency between us. You supported prostitution, I said something else. And Belén also argued. (Álvarez and Fernández 2021)*

In this interview, Lohana suggests that the television exposure achieved during that time forced them to discuss strategies for how to present their demands to the public. According to Berkins, the ATA members shied away from the idea of presenting themselves publicly as prostitutes, preferring to declare some 'honest' profession. Nadia maintained the position of presenting themselves as sex workers, because she and most of the members who followed her practiced sex work. Lohana had a more critical position that problematized the issue of sex work as an ultimate goal. The founders of ATA, María Belén Correa and Claudia Pía Baudracco, did not take a clear position on the issue and preferred to leave the debate outside their organization. They understood that there were other priority issues and that each of the members of the group could have different opinions without this causing political conflict.

These differences undermined alliances within the group, promoting its dissolution and then the establishment in 1997 of the Organization of Argentine Travestis and

Transsexuals, founded by Nadia Echazú, and the Association for the Struggle for Travesti and Transsexual Identity, founded by Lohana Berkins. Thus, the new landscape of travesti organizations was made up of three groups with different positions on the issue of sex work.

Following the critical events of 2001, the language of political demands will be articulated under new paradigms. The issues of human rights, memory, truth, and justice will be the main topics around which political demands will be constructed. In light of the significant policies enabled by the restart of trials for crimes against humanity, human rights organizations will carry out a series of actions that will allow the exercise of memory, reflection on the events that occurred during the dictatorship, and investigation into the crimes committed against those activists who lived their lives in opposition to the conservative values of the ecclesiastical-military government.

Although feminists and LGBT organizations were not directly included by these actions and discourses on memory, a reflection on the issue began to take shape within these spaces, aimed at considering the many issues that, despite democracy, had not been placed on the public agenda. The notion of the 'debt of democracy' emerged as a narrative in which various demands appear to be accepted. It serves to highlight the ongoing violence and segregation experienced by travestis, even within a democratic society. Lohana Berkins refers to this issue when she says about the events of the massive riots in December 2001: "And there were many of us travesti comrades who found ourselves in the Plaza de Mayo, with courage and determination we went out to defend a democracy that we have little part in." (Berkins 2008)

Abortion, sexual and reproductive health, sex education, marriage equality, violence against women, the gender identity law, etc. were identified as urgent issues that democratic governments had a 'duty' to address. The right to identity, in the case of travestis and trans people, emerged under the strengthening of a human rights paradigm and in line with demands for the restitution and identification of babies appropriated by the dictatorship. How is it possible to tell one's own story without an identity from which to declare oneself as part of the citizenry?

The recognition achieved by organizations representing travesti, transgender, and non-binary people by the state during the first decades of the 21st century is partly a victory and partly a resignation. To achieve its current status, the trans movement had to coordinate its demands with those of human rights organizations, feminists, LGBT organizations, political parties, etc. In this evolution of political agendas, where did the issue of sex work by travestis fit in?

*Political Struggle*

In 2004, Pelusa Liendro and Rosario Sansone, two travestis and sex workers, organized the first Pride Parade in the province of Salta. That first demonstration brought together a hundred travestis who worked the streets and were persecuted by the local police. During the march, Martha Cesar, leader of the Women's Multisectoral Group and a feminist journalist was interviewed and declared: "*There is no leader here like Lohana Berkins, who is a phenomenon. Note that when they reach a level of awareness about their situation within society, they abandon prostitution and turn to political struggle*"(Brizuela 2004)

This testimony makes it clear that, for some sectors of feminism, sex work and political action are two separate spheres, even irreconcilable to the extent that one must be abandoned in order to enter the other. This statement presents both spheres of action on a hierarchical plane, according to which 'prostitution' is inferior, undesirable, quasi-primitive, and 'political struggle' constitutes the universe of the desirable, the aspirational, the civilized. Although there is no systematization of public statements in this regard, there are testimonies about the perceptions that feminists had of trans women and travestis and their demands when they approached feminism. With the exception of Lohana Berkins and a few other trans activists, who early on managed to connect with the main leaders of Buenos Aires feminism and left-wing political parties, other travestis were only considered as objects of political demands, never as subjects with their own voices and experiences.

In order to achieve the current state of achievements of travesti and trans activism, it was also necessary to wage a political struggle within the alliances built between the LGBT movement, human rights organizations, and feminists. In this convergence of interests, the issue of sex work has been pushed aside on the agendas of today's activists. This omission is not because travestis have abandoned the activity or because the structural conditions of Argentine society today promote a reduction in the sex market. Prostitution, sex work, or whatever you want to call it, continues to be a topic of conversation among travestis, especially among the poorest migrants, outsiders of the political organizations. The bias introduced in the approach to the sex work, and the memory constructed about it, is framed by the mainstream political narrative, avoiding contradict the delicate agreements established between feminisms and sexual dissidents. That is why bills and political initiatives are aimed at introducing travestis into a life aligned with capitalist standards of human development. This is not entirely bad, as long as it does not obstruct those other options that, for better or worse, have served to develop travesti experiences. Ultimately, the material reproduction of life can, and even more so in the current paradigm of labor flexibility, be sustained between activities formally recognized as work and others considered complementary.

***

Déborah Singer was a highly popular travesti in the 1980s. She defined herself as an artist and was, in fact, one of the few recognized by the Variety Artists Union. Although show business was her world, she also worked on the streets. She never forgot her fellow travestis who accompanied her on the street, even when the flashes of photographers and the bright lights of television loved her. Deborah always remembered her street origins, her loving community of travestis. She knew how to use her fame to raise awareness of the crimes against travestis in Pan-American Highway during the harshest times of police repression. And although she claimed to be a sex worker and shamelessly displayed her erotic body, she was capable of political reflection on the issue of work, discrimination against travestis, and the need for deep changes in the moral standards of Argentine society.

In an interview in FLASH magazine on June 29, 1990, Deborah declared:

*There's nothing we can do about it, people like us have to go abroad to work. Here they treat us like animals. We're third-class citizens. We were screwed over by the military, and Raúl Alfonsín marginalized us incredibly too. And now, with the continuation of democracy, everything is the same. Just because I'm a travesti, it's not fair that no one wants to give me a job. I fought for freedom and human dignity. All those sacrifices didn't matter to me because I had hope that with democracy, better times would come. Look how wrong I was! Now the police don't beat us up as much, but the punishment comes in the form of work. It seems that those at the top have decided that people like us should starve to death. Ours is a country of retarded people, both in terms of laws and mentality. The issues of prostitution and homosexuality are still taboo. The media focuses on homosexuals and prostitution and ignores more important issues such as child hunger, poverty, and crime. When do we understand that in developed countries, issues related to sex have already been completely overcome? I am a die-hard fighter. I want to have a normal job, because when that happens, I will be able to be the person I want to be. For now, society is marginalizing me. I hope that one day the whole country will realize that travestis are not criminals, far from it. We are simply human beings seeking peace, land, and bread.*

The development of travesti and trans activism arrived on the Argentine political scene to challenge the most rigid conceptions of the sex-gender system, re-discuss the boundaries of sexual democracy, and propose new models of citizenship that are more heterogeneous and open to personal desire. Among their many demands, the end of police violence against travestis engaged in sex work was pretty important, not only because it was the banner of their public appearance, but also because sex work provided the mechanisms for encounter, dialogue, the production of demands, and the planning of actions. Paradoxically, the street was both the scene of extreme vulnerability and a trench for struggle and organization.

This is why this article draws attention to the constitution of notions about prostitution and sex work as two separate and irreconcilable spheres, and to the ways in which this dispute, which arose within feminism, spread to travesti organizations, shaping the production of memories that obliterate, silence, and block certain discourses that would contribute enormous richness to current debates. The current production of trans memory manages to recover from the past the experiences and trajectories of travestis whose main means of livelihood was the sex work, but the revision of that memory fails to reconcile the experience of the street with the organizational processes that occurred later. Conflicts over memory often express tensions and seek to construct victims and perpetrators, without taking into account that the traumatic events being remembered are imbued with nuances.

In this sense, revisiting the struggles of those travestis who took the first step by proudly positioning themselves as whores does not undermine current demands (Butierrez 2022). Reviewing these travesti memories reveals the depth of the organizational processes, the complexity of the social and political experience of travestis, and the richness that can be obtained from unbiased listening. Looking at the trajectories of travestis who have been unjustly marginalized from history allows us to appreciate the richness originally contained in their political narratives and to unravel possible actions that are essential to overcoming the seemingly strict boundary between abolitionism and regulationism.

After all, travestis are united by deeper experiences that transcend these conceptual discussions. Shared spaces, common trajectories, mischief, and playful humor are stronger than ideological and political differences. As Nadia Echazú said in that 2001 interview: *"The important thing to remember and emphasize is that, unlike all other communities, we have divided ourselves as an organization, but we have always worked as a group."*

# Trans Travesti Activism and Human Rights

# Justice from a Social Struggle Perspective: Travestis, Gays, and Lesbians in the Trial on Banfield and Quilmes Clandestine Detention Centers

What can be said about memory that hasn't been said before? In Argentina, we live moved by memory, immersed in a nostalgic spirit that binds us like the tango. We constantly immerse ourselves in commemorations and rituals, and we even inhabit the present with a certain historical awareness, knowing that we are part of moments, celebrations, and emotions that will be portrayed in books. There is a whole structure of monuments, memorials, and demarcations that support a national history mixed with big narratives and small stories and oral traditions. Over the last twenty years, memory has been a backbone of political life, and we have happily seen the portraits of repressors fall from the walls of the government buildings, the old detention centers converted into spaces of memory, and the struggle of mothers, grandmothers, and children of disappeared people commemorated in schools every March 24. But memory remained for a long time as a privilege limited to the cis-heterosexual nation. Only in the last decade projects have projects emerged to reconstruct the memory of travestis, transsexuals, gays, and lesbians. Archives, films, and research programs have forged a specific narrative to name the violence experienced by these groups, which no street names, monuments, or buildings commemorate.

Argentina is not just about memory. The axiom works by

linking memory with truth, and both with justice. Justice is one of the outstanding issues for travesti, trans, gay, and lesbian communities. Most, if not all, of the crimes committed against our identity and our desire are still part of democracy's great debt. Although efforts have been made in the academic world and in certain activist projects to characterize and represent the history of political violence against our communities, and although we have tried to put names on the graves of our comrades, we are still far from achieving justice and reparation for the torture, abuse, murders, and illegal detentions committed by the military dictatorship against trans and queer people. Fortunately, little by little, windows of opportunity have been opening through which justice sheds light on the truth and attempts to compensate the victims.

In 2018, in the province of Santa Fe, a group of ten trans women and travestis, through an original interpretation of the provincial law that stipulates reparations for victims of the dictatorship, obtained a reparatory pension that not only allows them to access minimum living conditions, but also recognizes the state's responsibility for the violence they suffered. In 2020, Valeria del Mar Ramirez was the first trans woman to be a plaintiff in a trial on crimes against humanity and to offer her testimony about the violence she experienced during her detention in the Banfield clandestine detention center. Also in 2020, the Ministry of Justice and Human Rights recognized Karina Pintarelli as a victim of the systematic persecution carried out by the civil-military dictatorship against trans people and more recently stipulated that she should receive a pension similar to the one for former political prisoners. In 2022, Fabiana Gutierrez and Julieta "La Trachyn" Gonzalez also received historic reparations from the government of the province of Buenos Aires, after being recognized as victims of violence in clandestine detention centers. These few precedents represent small but significant steps forward in transcending memory and building justice for the travesti and trans community.

Among these significant efforts, the judicial process accompanying the trial investigating the crimes of the clandestine centers from Banfield and Quilmes promises to be the first ones to record the systematic violence against travestis, transsexuals, lesbians, and gays and the participation of the military forces in these crimes oriented to discipline sexuality. This trial began in October 2020 and featured the testimony of Valeria del Mar Ramírez as the only trans plaintiff, but in 2022, the testimonies of seven other travestis and trans people were added as plaintiffs. The inclusion of these eight trans victims in the trial will set a significant precedent in the state's recognition of the systematic plan of repression against the LGBT community during the last dictatorship, but it will also establish the future responsibility of the state and the police in the continuation of this violence in democratic times.

The Investigation

Prosecutor Ana Oberlín is a key figure in this investigation. Her doctoral thesis focused on the violence suffered by travestis and trans people during the last dictatorship, and she is familiar with previous research on this subject. Her appointment as prosecutor in this trial allowed her to include the cases of travestis and trans people in the indictment and to bring a gender perspective to this case. Judicial investigation has different characteristics from the intellectual approaches with which social science researchers can often understand certain historical events. Here, the aim is to prove facts and secure convictions against the perpetrators, and to do so, cases must be built with determination and without leaving room for doubt. Oberlín aims to clarify three central issues: 1- violence against the LGBT community intensified during the dictatorship; 2- the perpetrators were military personnel and used a specific method of detention and torture; sexual violence was perpetrated; and 3- the victims shared detention spaces with cisgender detainees and disappeared people. With this strategy, the prosecution hopes to obtain convictions and find a way for recognition and financial compensation from the state.

Academic research on this issue has led to different conclusions. For some researchers, it is impossible to compare the violence against the LGBT community with that suffered by labor, student, and left-wing activists during the dictatorship, because while the latter were subjected to torture, clandestine detention, and disappearance using particularly cruel techniques; travestis, transsexuals, gays, and lesbians suffered a different type of violence that did not generally lead to physical disappearance. In many cases, this idea is reinforced by its temporal dimension, because the persecution, detention, and punishment of sexuality is previous to the dictatorship and extends beyond its end. Furthermore, the violence against trans and queer people was supported by laws, edicts, and misdemeanor codes enacted under democratic governments that were in force from the 1930s until the end of the 20th century. There are also investigations and interviews with activists from the

Homosexual Liberation Front, which show that the repressive forces targeted political dissent rather than sexual dissent. There has also been widespread debate regarding the number of 400 LGBT disappeared persons. On the other hand, there is research that fervently defends the hypothesis that the LGBT community was a target of extermination carried out by the military juntas, basing their accusation on testimonies, documents, and memoirs that record the systematic and specific nature of the violence during this period. This second line of thinking is supported by the work of Oberlín and other specialists who have been called as witnesses in the trial of the Banfield, Quilmes, and Lanús clandestine detention centers.

In her article Trans women and travestis: a great debt to pay for a better democracy, recently published by the Center for Legal and Social Studies, Ana Oberlín states that:

*What happened [to travestis, trans women, lesbians, and gay men] during the years of state terrorism was that this violence intensified. Furthermore, this intensification focused particularly on trans women and travestis who, almost without exception, were involved in street prostitution and, for that reason, were more exposed to attacks by the repressive forces. In addition to the daily state violence, they suffered the mechanisms of state terrorism: they were forcibly disappeared and taken to various clandestine detention, torture, and extermination centers, where they were subjected to continuous torture with particular cruelty. In addition to their persecution by the police, who had always been responsible for their repression, other groups belonging to the armed and security forces, including civilian members, also took part in these acts during those years (Oberlin 2022).*

These simple but effective foundations underpin the prosecution's accusations in the case. Without the delays, nuances, and twists and turns that history researchers tend to use to complicate the analyses, Oberlin's investigation, based on the testimonies of trans women and travestis, allows for a clear characterization of the violence during that period. The eight plaintiffs agree that they were detained by the military, taken to clandestine detention centers, and sexually assaulted. In that context, they suffered a specific type of violence that was different from what they experienced before and after the dictatorship in the dungeons of democracy.

*Expert Witnesses*

On Tuesday, March 14, 2024 Dr. Flavio Rapisardi testified in the court as an expert witness in order to reinforce the idea of the systematic and specific nature of military violence against LGBT people. During his testimony, he explained the research process he carried out as a member of the Center for Queer and Multicultural Studies at the University of Buenos Aires, which led to the publication of "*Fiestas, Baños y Exilios: Los Gays Porteños en la última dictadura*" [Parties, Bathrooms, and Exiles]. Gays during the last military dictatorship], co-authored with Alejandro Modarelli. This text is a classic in Argentine LGBT literature and a reference text for those who reflect on the violence during the dictatorship. In his statement, Rapisardi pointed out that, following the proposal of renowned historian specialized in genocide Daniel Feierstein, they identified that the military dictatorship operated according to a system that began with the targetting of LGBT individuals, continued with the effective identification of that group, and culminated in extermination, which could be genocidal or gradual.

*"Many of the testimonies we collected during our investigation date back to 1975, shortly after Perón's death. During those years, the emergence of the Argentine Anticommunist Alliance began to shape the image of an internal enemy. In El Caudillo magazine, directed by then-Minister López Rega, they published an illustration entitled "The Tree of Subversion", showing a tree with revolutionary groups such as the Revolutionary Army of the People (ERP) as roots and the term HOMOSEXUALITY, now out of fashion, as branches. This marked a sector of the population identified as the enemy,"* Rapisardi stated.

Their research involved between 150 and 170 interviews with different LGBT people who lived during the dictatorship and allowed them to characterize spaces and practices of sociability that served as refuges from state violence. The existence of these specific practices of sociability, which Rapisardi and Modarelli identify as beginning in 1976 and not before, reflects the increase in systematic violence by the military juntas against the gay community. These clandestine meeting places were invented in response to the growing moral panic fueled by the media affiliated with the repressive forces around the danger of the 'homosexual subject.'

In his testimony, Rapisardi pointed out that this system of parties, bathrooms, and exile was identified and dismantled by security forces, especially through the use of intelligence services that closely investigated the activities of gays and lesbians in these places. The bathrooms at train stations, which run through the Buenos Aires suburbs and the federal capital, were subject to surveillance and repression. They had already been formally regulated during the administration of Commissioner Margaride (during the Onganía government), who ordered their closure; but since the last dictatorship, many officers entered the bathrooms dressed in civilian clothes to gather intelligence. Once there, they had sex with homosexuals whom they identified, persecuted, and arrested. This action constitutes a type of sexual violence that was often repeated in police stations and detention centers. This reinforces the thesis that violence against the LGBT community during the dictatorship was not only carried out by the regular police, but that other security and intelligence services also took part in these actions. It also reveals a specific way of identifying and punishing sexual dissidence that had not occurred previously.

Rapisardi also reported that detainees were placed in small closets where they were physically abused and insulted and forced to stand in unsanitary conditions without food or access to a bathroom for more than 24 hours. Most of the time, part of this torture involved publicly exposing the detainees' homosexuality, as security forces would call the detainees' family members and/or employers to reveal their sexual orientation. Travestis were also tortured and detained for much longer periods of time, as their family members rarely came to claim them. Their class status and the marginality of their street experience led travestis to be subjected to brutal violence. They were practically hunted down on the roads and in areas of sex work to be kidnapped and sexually assaulted, sometimes at the hands of the military or other common detainees. In his statement,

Flavio Rapisardi also addressed the issue of the 400 disappeared:

> "At that time, and here we have the testimonies of Carlos Jáuregui and other activists, there was an attempt to approach those who were part of CONADEP, and the only one who agreed to answer questions was Rabbi Marshall Meyer, who, when asked whether or not they were leaving data on the sexual orientation the gender identity of the people who had been kidnapped in the clandestine torture and extermination centers of the Argentine Republic, said that they had not reached an agreement. Marshall Meyer agreed that a trace of this would be left in the testimonies and said something that still resonates with us today: In all the testimonies that I was part of and heard as part of CONADEP, I can conclude that lesbians, gays, trans people, people with disabilities, and Jewish people were tortured in particular. I do not want to generate a discussion about degrees of torture, but I understand that Rabbi Meyer is referring to violence against groups that were already vulnerable, where stereotypes were reinforced and where, in addition to electric prods and beatings, there was cruelty based on their ethnic or religious origin or sexual identity. Due to the fear of other CONADEP members of creating divisions among the victims of the dictatorship, this specific lead indicated by Meyer was set aside."

Rapisardi's testimony is extremely useful in characterizing the climate of repression against lesbians, gays, and trans people during 1976-1983. His research, based on interviews and written documents, provides an intellectual framework for the prosecution's case. Similarly, historian Ana Cecilia Solari Paz, a researcher of the Provincial Commission for

Memory's Research and Memory Sites Program, has been summoned to testify in the near future. Her research work "aMorales *en dictadura*" [(Im)Morals in the Dictatorship] draws on a documentary survey of the archives of the Intelligence Division of the Buenos Aires Provincial Police to examine the mechanisms of persecution and repression deployed by the security forces between 1976 and 1983 (Solari Paz 2023). It is an intense work of archival exploration that reveals the police structure responsible for the registration, persecution, and punishment of those who did not conform to the Catholic sexual morality of the military government.

*Justice for reparation*

Foucault says that "*Rather than thinking of the social struggle in terms of 'justice', one has to emphasise justice in terms of the social struggle.*" Justice is a field of enormous dispute, always crossed by ideals and ideologies. The French philosopher highlights the role that judicial institutions play in social struggles, both in repressing them and in encouraging their development (Chomsky and Foucault 2006). The trial of the 17 defendants charged with crimes committed in the Banfield and Quilmes clandestine detention centers is an example of how to achieve justice from the perspective of social struggle. The prosecution team led by Ana Oberlín is actively committed to the victims of the repressive system of the military juntas and is strongly committed to documenting a specific type of violence that has in many cases been overlooked. The cis-hetero-centered justice system has always acted in a monolithic manner, prioritizing its own class and gender interests and dismissing any minor fracture that could undermine its arguments. But this prosecutor's office has cast aside all fear and ventured to build a case that includes these other forms of violence, which until now had only been discussed in academic circles and among trans and queer activists.

The participation of researchers from the field of social sciences in this judicial process highlights the political dimension of the search for truth. It is not just a matter of accumulating documents and testimonies, producing complex analyses, and filling pages of academic papers, but rather of producing knowledge that is committed to the community and whose usefulness allows us to access rights that have historically been denied. The work of Rapisardi and Solari Paz, as well as that of Oberlín, transcends mere analysis and provides the framework for identifying the criminal actions of the security forces during the last dictatorship. It is a surface from which to leap over the debts of democracy. The work of this prosecutor's office aims not only to secure convictions for past crimes, but also to set a legal precedent that will serve as jurisprudence for future lawsuits against the various security forces that, both in democracy and under dictatorships, have been the killers of our comrades. It also offers strong arguments for the fight for a law of historical reparation for the trans community, which has been waiting too long.

Researchers and judicial officials on both sides of the wall can (and must) break through the established meanings of dictatorial violence until we dig a tunnel that connects us and allows our perspectives to intertwine with those of trans and queer activists. This operation of rupture and encounter is the only way to put the memories in action, bring them together to produce truths, and allow us to achieve justice and historical reparation for the LGBT community, which has been harshly denied after forty years of democracy.

# A Century of Violence Against Trans Bodies: A New Chronology for Reparation Policies

Over the past five years, LGBTIQ+ and feminist groups have worked intensively to construct a narrative about gay, lesbian, and trans victims during the last military dictatorship. This intellectual and activist effort to demand recognition and justice for detainees and disappeared members of the 'LGBT community ' [7]has not been free of tensions and questions. On the one hand, it has been extremely difficult to document the existence of a systematic plan to exterminate sexual dissidents carried out by the military junta, but it has also been problematic to inquire about the sexuality of detainees and disappeared people who were mainly involved in activism in unions, political parties, and students organizations.

One of the most consistent criticisms on this issue was made by sociologist Joaquín Insausti, who pointed out the difficulties in confirming the existence of a systematic plan to exterminate the LGBT population, although the existence of long-term violence based on other mechanisms of state control over sexuality cannot be denied (Insausti 2015). In his article, Insausti explores various testimonies

---

[7] It is difficult to use the term "LGBT community" as such during this period, since collective groups of gay men, lesbians, bisexuals, and trans people would not emerge until the mid-1990s. Regarding the terminology and categories used in the text, I will occasionally use some contemporary terms to refer to past experiences, but generally, I will use the categories native to and specific to each time period in order to remain faithful to the specific ways of naming things in each era.

and documents that show that although there were members of the Homosexual Liberation Front (FLH) who experienced persecution, detention, and violence during the last years of Peronism and the beginning of the military dictatorship, this was not a direct result of their homosexual activism (which was largely kept secret) but rather their participation in trade unions and left-wing political groups. Similarly, he points out that anti-LGBT violence did not stop with the advent of democracy, but rather reorganized itself in response to the police force's need to raise dirty money through bribery and the exploitation of sex work zones.

In this text, I aim to insert into this complex field of debates some voices and perspectives focused on the experience of travestis and transsexuals, in order to break down the specificities of state violence against dissident ways of embodying gender. The issue has been extensively addressed by activists and intellectuals from the gay community, but only a few travesti and transsexual voices have articulated the specific ways in which the last military dictatorship disciplined trans bodies. Historical difficulties in accessing higher education and academic spaces have meant that trans voices have been heard as oral testimony and as a miscellany attached to the complaints of gays and lesbians, but the specific dimensions of violence against the trans community have rarely been addressed from a scientific perspective. Therefore, it is necessary to incorporate a perspective from trans studies that proposes thinking about violence from the experience of those who inhabited a non-normative body and transgressed gender boundaries, to complement the approach that studies on sexualities have already taken around sexual orientation as the axis of oppression and violence.

The emergence in recent years of demands for reparations policies for the travesti trans population alert about the need to rethink the characteristics of the violence that the Argentine state has deployed against travestis and transsexuals; during which periods such violence took place; and on what legal and narratives the control of sexualities was structured. To answer these questions, this text will begin by investigating the origin of the legal instruments that regulated the offering of sex in public spaces and the wearing of clothing contrary to one's sex during the first half of the 20th century. I will then analyze the legal restrictions that made it impossible for transsexuals to access 'sex change' surgeries and get their gender recognized on identification documents. Finally, I will reconstruct the violence that occurred from the return of democracy in 1983 until the constitutional reform of 1994 on the Pan-American Highway and other red-light districts. The ultimate goal will be to expose how the Argentine state constructed a surveillance mechanism that combined legal and medical instruments, police practices, and social narratives to regulate any type of transgression of the standards of biological sexual binaryism and conservative morality.

*Legal Instruments for Controlling Sexuality: Ordinances 2H and 2F*

Issue No. 2 of Postdata magazine, the publication of the Gay Federation Group published in October 1984, reproduces an article by Néstor Perlongher, previously published in Persona magazine, edited by feminist activist Maria Elena Oddone. Under the title "About some ordinances,"

Perlongher reconstructs a brief history of violence against homosexuals and sex workers justified by the code of misdemeanors censoring "scandal." In this curious text, Perlongher establishes a continuum of repression of sexuality that began with Peronism, deepened during Frondizism, and escalated to its maximum expression during the last military dictatorship. Perlongher emphasizes the ordinance known as 2H, which punishes the offering or incitement of "carnal acts." The text mentions several dates that the author considers central to the constitution of this "jungle of ordinances." First, he points to the drafting of the Regulations on Misdemeanor Procedures, approved by Perón through Decree 10.868/46, which gives the Federal Police the authority to intervene in the punishment of minor offenses through the issuance of daily ordinances and empowers the Chief of Police to act as a judge. He then mentions the existence of ordinance 2H (established in the daily ordinances of April 19, 1949), which punishes "persons of either sex who publicly incite or offer themselves for carnal acts." Perlongher also mentions the existence of other ordinances aimed at punishing sexual freedoms:

> "Similarly, subsection "F" punishes 'exhibiting oneself in public places or public spaces dressed or disguised in clothing of the opposite sex'; and subsection "I": 'being found in the company of a minor under the age of 18 when known to be a pervert' (daily ordinances of June 15, 1932). [...] Other provisions punish 'indecent' clothing and were used to arrest men wearing tank tops, shorts, or bare chests, women wearing miniskirts, etc."

In this way, Perlongher reunited a group of extremely

diverse legal instruments implemented by the Argentine state since 1946. He insists on pointing out Peronism's responsibility for the repression of dissident sexualities, when later in the text he notes the arrest of "immoral" individuals during the campaign for the reopening of brothels, whose absence was considered the cause of the proliferation of the homosexual plague. He also highlights how these police ordinances served as a platform for repression during the governments of Frondizi, Onganía, and María Estela Martínez de Perón.

From current research by Cristiana Schettini and Diego Galeano, we know that the legal mechanisms for controlling sexual morality in Argentina have a complex origin dating back to the second half of the 19th century, when the nascent police force debated the controversy on prostitution (Galeano and Schettini 2022). At the beginning of the 20th century, the municipal police were responsible for ensuring hygiene and prophylaxis in brothels, but little by little a 'morality police'[8] was established, interfering in private matters such as young girls running away from home, domestic conflicts, marital dramas, and scandalous sexual behavior. From this tangle of police practices, "public morality" divisions or brigades were formed, and around 1932, during the period known as the infamous decade[9], the first drafts of edicts 2°H and 2°F were produced, key legal instruments for controlling 'scandal,' transvestism, prostitution, and homosexuality. In short, these ordinances

---

[8] Morality squads or brigades existed throughout Argentina. A detailed study of the existence of these brigades and their record-keeping and criminal record practices sheds light on the growing state concern with morality and sexual health by the 1930s.

[9] The period between the 1930 coup d'état and 1943 is known as the infamous decade due to the extremist conservative policies developed by the military dictators and the economic crisis.

represent the mechanism through which police control of sexual morality in Argentina was articulated from the 1930s to the end of the 20th century.[10]

**The Argentine Government Against 'Sex Change' Surgeries.**

"The brown-skinned woman, who was physically robust, appeared to be around 40 years old, which could be verified in the documents she presented with a determined gesture; only in the papers, the woman's face, undoubtedly the same face, was a masculine one, under which was written Mauro Fernando Vega, born in Andalgalá, Catamarca. Mauro wanted to be called María Fernanda, because she had changed a lot in recent times. Civil judge Bunge Campos did not grant the woman's request to have all her names feminized. Ten forensic doctors examined the petitioner; the examination showed that, in fact, there was no error in the documents. Mauro Fernando Vega was a grown man, castrated and emasculated. Bunge Campos ordered an investigation and referred the case to the criminal court, in case there had been a crime."

A few days later, a doctor from Caballito made a curious complaint at police station 49: the male teacher at a local dance academy, which was attended by many minors, had become a female teacher. Arrested by the police, the dancer Ricardo Armesto stated that he had his sexual organs removed by the surgeon Francisco Defazio, and that another

---

[10] There is a significant gap in the historical record for the period 1935–1955, which coincides with the second half of the "infamous decade" and the first two Peronist administrations. Newspaper records document the turbulent political life of the time, but they scarcely reflect the sex scandals (with the exception of a few examples). A more detailed study of this period might reveal other practices of sexual control, such as confinement in prisons and psychiatric hospitals.

*prestigious surgeon, Dr. Pavlosky, had created an artificial vagina for him through a complex plastic surgery operation. A few weeks later, it became known that Mauro Vega had also been operated on by Defazio. Lindor Vega joined these two men. Defazio, according to reports at the time, had transformed him into the young and attractive Liliana Vega. The tabloid press viciously attacked the surgeons and their patients: without knowing who or how many they were, or what the transformation consisted of, morbid publicity spread about the matter. The "men-women" (hombre-mujer) ended up winning, integrating into society and insisting on identifying themselves as authentic examples of the female sex. (Hanglin & Santagada, 1966)*

This is how the April 1966 issue of Panorama magazine portrayed the scandalous emergence of numerous cases of 'men-women' who, through surgeries performed by Dr. Francisco Defazio, demanded to be recognized by the Argentine state as legitimate women. This episode marked a turning point in the medical and legal management of sex in Argentina. First, the courts arrested the doctors who performed these surgeries, arguing that they had castrated their patients without any therapeutic purpose. The legal persecution of this prestigious group of surgeons served as a disciplinary message for the medical community, which for the next three decades would permanently refuse to perform any type of procedure aimed at modifying 'biological' sex. Furthermore, this event led to the intervention of criminal justice in medical decisions regarding sex organs in general.

The commotion caused by the arrest of Clemente Rodríguez Jáuregui, Alejandro Pavlosky, Ricardo San Martín, and

Francisco Defazio led to the political decision to pass a new version of the Medical Practice Act in 1967. Article 20, paragraph 18, establishes the prohibition of *"performing interventions that cause sterilization without a clearly determined therapeutic indication and without having exhausted all conservative resources for the reproductive organs."* This legislation, passed and promulgated by the military dictator Juan Carlos Onganía, will primarily restrict access to 'sex change' surgeries for transsexual people, but it will also prevent the plasticity of sex and people's self-determination over their reproductive capacity from being questioned.

In addition to these restrictions, the justice system will systematically refuse to recognize the gender of those who manage to rectify their 'sex,' arguing that only nature and God can determine such matters. It will not be until 1996, with the recognition of Mariela Muñoz, that the justice system will make progress on the issue and recognize, partially, trans citizenship.

*Destape*[11] *Travesti: Violence During the Democratic Spring*

Between 1983 and 1993, the sensationalist media focused its attention on the paradisiacal world of travestis built along the Pan-American Highway. The international highway was a bustling nightlife scene where the first red-light district of travestis was established. The advent of democracy brought with it the possibility of openly exhibiting these novel bodies, which, through the use of self-administered hormones and silicone implants, were able to transgress the

[11] *El Destape* [the unveiling] was a period marked by the acceptance of erotic and sexual artistic content immediately following the end of the dictatorship. A similar phenomenon occurred in Spain after the Franco regime ended.

gender barriers imposed by the medical-legal system in Argentina. However, the representation of travestis in the local print media was tinged with blood. Amidst the bright and heated showbiz stories and morbid reports about this unprecedented 'third sex,' there was a string of murders and accidental deaths involving the travestis of Pan-American Highway. There were even suspicions of a serial killer known as 'the butterfly hunter.'

The truth is that the fanciful narrative of the butterfly hunter only served to sell magazines and absolve the Argentine state of its responsibility for the largest massacre of travestis. Although there are not many details regarding the number of victims, and reconstructing it documentarily is still a challenge, it would not be difficult to estimate more than one hundred deaths of travestis in Pan-American Highway and other red-light districts around the city of Buenos Aires. There are various reasons why travestis were persecuted during this period, but all of them are linked to the existence of an organized legal and social apparatus to punish sexual freedoms and the transgression of gender binarism. As I have pointed out so far, a series of police ordinances were the scaffolding for the police persecution of travestis and transsexuals, but the boom in Pan-American Highway was also marked by the practice of sex work. Thus, police chiefs in the adjacent neighborhoods enforced both 2H and 2F to arrest them, although not always for moral misbehaviours. Persecution during the period 1983-1993 often functioned as a way of collecting bribes to swell the petty cash of police stations. In many cases, travestis reached agreements with the police, but these became weak when they had to 'make statistics,' that is, present a minimum number of arrests of offenders to the authorities;

or when the notoriety of the scandal encouraged neighbors to demand an increase in raids.

Following the privatization of Pan-AmericanHighway in 1993 and the work to expand it, red-light districts moved to other spaces, this time within the City of Buenos Aires (Alvarez 2017), which was undergoing a process of autonomy and drafting its own statutes[12]. However, edicts 2F and 2H continued to enforced, at least until 1999/2003 a repressive system that combined social terror in the face of the sexual disruption imposed by travestis, police corruption, and the growing narrative of sexual prophylaxis in the face of the advance of the 'gay plague'.[13]

*Chronologies of Violence Against Travestis and Transsexuals*

Although it is not incorrect to assert, as some current political projects do, that violence against the travesti and trans population increased during the last military dictatorship or that during this period the repressive forces of the police and military were mobilized to persecute sexual dissidents, it is not possible to reduce the history of violence against 'sexual difference' to a genealogy limited to the debate between dictatorship and democracy. A review of the documentary sources produced by the Argentine state on the issue of sexuality reveals at least three fundamental

[12] The Constitutional Convention of the City of Buenos Aires, which began its work in July 1996, repealed police ordinances and established less restrictive regulations regarding sex work in the City of Buenos Aires; however, these laws underwent a series of advances and setbacks until 2003, and in practice, trans women continued to be arrested for soliciting sex, causing a public disturbance, and other misdemeanors.

[13] The role of narratives surrounding the HIV/AIDS epidemic in the repressive actions and murders of transgender women still warrants a detailed study, but there are some documentary records in which neighbors, officials, and police personnel highlight the danger posed by transgender women as a vector for the spread of the disease.

issues: 1) the state permanently regulated all sexual behavior that was outside of heterosexual sex for reproductive purposes; 2) it implemented a system of legal and medical instruments of varying scope against any exercise of sexuality that would cause "scandal"; and 3) these instruments transcended the upheavals of political life, functioning as a device for controlling sexuality during both democratic and dictatorial governments. Furthermore, it is feasible to assert that the state's vocation for controlling sexuality has remained uninterrupted over time, at least from the beginning of the 20th century to the first decades of the 21st century, although the intensity and strategies of its policies have changed during the governments that have succeeded one another for almost a century.

This text does not seek to dismantle the claims made by trans activism regarding violence during the last military dictatorship, but rather to extend the discussion to democratic periods and demonstrate that violence against travestis and transsexuals is sustained by a long-standing medical, legal, and political structure that was established alongside the Argentine state and the professionalization of the police and military forces. In this way, I aim to compel democracy and the Argentine state to take responsibility for the debt it owes to the trans population, which transcends the small number of survivors of the military dictatorship. The victims of this system of sexual surveillance number in the thousands and include all expressions of the trans population, but also all bodies that transgressed heterosexual sex for reproductive purposes, from homosexuals to cisgender female sex workers.

Therefore, policies for reparation and compensation for the travesti and trans population should not be limited to the period of the last military dictatorship, but should also include the years before and after it, when travestis and transsexual people were subjected to repression, detention, and exile due to police edicts and laws prohibiting 'sex change.' Even today, there are still provinces that uphold ordinances and misdemeanor codes that, under the guise of prohibiting the offering of sex in public places or causing a scandal, continue to persecute, detain, displace, and disappear travestis and trans people. Although 40 years have passed since the restoration of democracy, it is only in the last decade that travestis, transsexuals, trans men, and non-binary people have begun to be considered part of the citizenry, and there are still obstacles to accessing justice, health care, education, employment, the right to the city, and so many other spheres. A hundred years of repressive sexuality policies continue to operate in state practices and forms of surveillance. Only a thorough, critical, and in-depth examination of the history of the Argentine state will allow us to reformulate its current practices, to free trans bodies from the guardianship, pity, and domestication imposed by the cis-hetero-patriarchal dictatorship.

# A Kiss to the Sky for Those Who Are No Longer with Us

*This was the first dress I wore outside, on an important birthday. March 3, between Florida and Maipú... there I was. So, I got out of the taxi, I walked two meters and I noticed a Fiat van, usually the car that undercover cops used. It hit me, you know, the Fiat van. I didn't want it to hit me, because I was going to a birthday party. I was dressed up and I was happy. I started hitting them, scratching them all. They threw me to the ground, ripped my dress off, and when I fell, I had blue shoes. I hit him on the forehead with them so he would let me go. And people surrounded us: "Leave her alone, leave her alone..." they shouted. Then they handcuffed me and took me away. Goodbye dress and goodbye birthday!"*

This short story of Vanesa Flawer is how any trans genealogy could begin. A scene from everyday life brutally interrupted by violence. However, writing a history about travestis requires a different intellectual effort. A history about travestis needs new chronologies, new narrative strategies, and a lot of patience. To make trans history we need to untangle a web of intertwined anecdotes, a crossroads of perspectives that still sparks discussions among our community today. All travestis like to be protagonists, and sometimes history is not trained to listen to so many voices. Historiography constructs structures that organize history into winners and losers, and above all, into voices and silences. Although in recent years the totalizing attitude of history has given way to small narratives produced from lower levels, to black, feminist, and other memories, historicizing the 'trans issue' remains a contradictory challenge. At the same time that we need a progressive chronology that denounces the past in order to imagine a present, all travesti stories escape and resist being organized.

On this challenging path of constructing a history of travestis, two obstacles that we must urgently solve are chronologies and categories. Every article written about travesti experiences presents periods and descriptions that limit the object of research. Although this operation is necessary when stating a history, it is absurd when investigating it. If our research aims to find certain current identity configurations in historical records, we will always navigate pristine waters, but the challenge is to sink into the murky ones. Trans studies in the region continually insist on pointing to the emergence of travestis in the 1960s as a consequence of the spread of hormone therapies. Prior to this period, the recorded cases are thought of in other categories, such as transformists associated with the world of entertainment or as travesti expressions limited to carnival. Our existence has also been thought of as a progression from gays to travestis, which, although it attempts to draw guidelines for a common emotional community, reinforces a view of trans identity and sexual desire that assumes similarities between practices and life projects that are far from comparable. All these ways of thinking about trans aim to construct something pristine, clear definitions that allow us to understand and find trans people in moments and places.

All these definitions have constrained our understanding

and rendered our field of research useless. In recent years, there has been a proliferation of works that scrutinize travesti experiences in uncreative places and periods. Many research projects seek out travestis in carnivals, in journalistic discourse, in medical records, and on magazine billboards. Travestis as objects, travestis as victims. This static subject, monitored by the discourses of science, art, and the state, is comfortable and easy to grasp. To this we must add the problem of chronologies. Many works associate travesti experiences with classic periods such as el destape [*the unveiling*], the democratic transition, the coup d'état, or the first Peronism. Everyone forgets to imagine that perhaps travestis inhabited the unveiling before the first breasts appeared on television or that democracy did not begin with Alfonsín for travesti people. If we do not find travestis in other places and times, it does not mean that they did not exist, but rather that we are looking for them through the wrong lens. Perhaps if we really looked against the grain, even against our own ideology, we could see that 'transvestism' began much earlier than we think and inhabited many more spaces than just the metropolis.

As a counterpart to these limitations, travesti and trans archives are currently venturing possible answers. Without the pretensions of queer theory and with little more than the tools of intuition, travestis are recovering stories and organizing them into trans memory archives. From an emotional politics, the travesti community gathers the stories of their friends through uncertain clippings. Each photo brings with it hypothesis and fantasy. There are no truths or lies, only memories. Although each documentary collection bears the name of the person who donated the material, the ownership of that memory belongs to everyone. These sets of photographs are also a list of the names of friends, traveling companions, hotel mates, and silicone sisters. The archive is animated by the duty of memory, by the desire to honor those who are absent, and demand justice for them.

Regional Memories

Since the founding of the Trans National Memory Archive, the issue of travel and exile has been a central topic. Perhaps the influence of a tireless nomad like Claudia Pia Baudracco has left a rarely addressed mark: the issue of travesti mobility. Baudracco was responsible for the territorial expansion of the Association of Travestis, Transgender, and Transsexuals of Argentina (ATTTA), as she personally visited every corner of the country, spreading interest in the organization. She traveled across all landscapes, using the most vehicles. She boarded old long-distance buses to visit every province where she knew a colleague and traveled through northern Argentina on a small motorcycle, like a travesti Che Guevara. This wanderlust encouraged her to promote a project even bigger than ATTTA, which today has local incarnations: the archives.

In recent years, travesti and trans archives have transcended the borders of Buenos Aires. Among the many regional projects, the Travesti and Trans Memory Archive of Santa Fe stands out for the close link between the archival project and the community's demand for historical reparation for the trans community. In Santa Fe, there are twenty travesti and trans women who have received pensions from the provincial government, which recognizes the repressive actions of the state. Two of these women, Carolina Boetti and Marzia Echenique, are leading the Archive project, which currently not only collects photographs but also produces audiovisual documentaries based on the testimonies of travestis, addressing different topics from an original perspective: exile, confinement, memory, shows, humor, etc.

The Travesti and Trans Memory Archive project in Santa Fe is made up of Carolina and Marzia, as well as Karla Ojeda and several collaborators who work on recording and digitizing. During a recent visit, I was able to talk and record some anecdotes and experiences for future research on the intersections between trans memory, archive production, and struggles for human rights recognition. Carolina is an actress and was the first trans woman to receive compensation from the provincial government. Karla is a prominent member of the trans local community and the 'Trans-Knowledges' Program at the National University of Rosario.

Reparation came in May 2018 through a judicial appeal, which invoked an existing law to compensate victims of state terrorism and was applied to the cases of the travestis. The path to reparation began with an investigation of archives. Carolina and her lawyers collected a large number of documents from court files that attested to the persecution she had suffered at the hands of the police's public morality division and confirmed the long periods of confinement that exceeded 120 days.

> *"There were ten of us who started out, all of us had lived through the dictatorship. At that time, we were a collective of 40 trans women, of whom 10 are still alive. The others, unfortunately, all died along the way. Those of us who remain knew each other very well because in those years we*

*lived in a community, we lived in boarding houses. There was a very strong bond between us because there was no other choice. We helped each other."*

The lawsuit also included statements from cisgender victims of the dictatorship who attested to having been imprisoned alongside travestis. This is because detention facilities for travestis and political dissidents were shared. Peak H, where the homosexual wing was located in the third floor of the police headquarters where 'special units' operated, and the 4th police station were just some of the detention centers. Among the projects being carried out by the Archive is the declaration of the third-floor offices of the headquarters as a space of memory. They still visit these sites with emotion, searching for the documents they need for the trials against the state. Carolina vividly remembers the detention spaces and the harsh conditions: *"You were detained all the time. We would go out in the morning and at night, and they would catch us again and put us back in detention for 120 days, and so on and so forth. Out of the whole year, we were free for one month."*

Constant confinement, police harassment, and limited opportunities for social advancement were some of the reasons why travestis migrated to Europe. Carolina lived abroad from 1987 to 2009. Today, she refers to that period as exile, but at the time, it was the usual lifeline among them.

It was the only option we had at the time; we had no other choice. We lived here completely... We lived in boarding houses and couldn't get ahead financially. We were always a group that was severely punished by everyone. In the boarding houses, they charged us three times more than what they charged supposedly 'normal' people. We went out to work at night, and they detained us the whole time. When we came back, we would return to the boarding houses and find that everything had been stolen, or we would always be in debt. Our lives were full of suffering and pain; it was like being trapped in a hole with no way out. Well, the first ones to go into exile were Betiana Tuzzio and Emilia Antonelli, and we, who were closer at the time, would send each other money for the trip. First, one would leave, work, and then send the money for the other to pay for her ticket. I arrived, worked, paid back the money, and sent it to another, and so on. It was a whole chain; we helped each other. That was the only way we could leave; there was no other way.

These collective approaches to building care networks and survival strategies were central to travestis at that time and were reconfigured with each passing decade. Karla did not experience the military dictatorship, but violence against travestis transcends the boundaries between dictatorships and democracies. Her activism began in the 1990s, inspired by Lohana Berkins and other activists who, from television screens and street riots, stirred up trans pride.

> Watching Mauro Viale's TV show and seeing the travestis who participated in it and presented their collective demands, we understood that this was the way forward. It wasn't about the prettiest dress or the most splendid surgery. It was about having an organized and collective struggle. In that sense, in 1998, after two years of arrests that we were already fed up with, we decided to report the police who were taking bribes in the red-light district. We denounced the police chief. We made the complaints at the 5th and 4th police stations, which were on the border, separated from each other by an avenue. If you crossed over to one side, it was the 4th, and on the other side, it was the

*5th, and that sometimes saved us from being arrested. The six or seven of us organized a riot, and then we went as a group to report the brigade or the command that was there at the time. The chief at the time was Benedicto de Matias. We denounced him and managed to get it in the media. Then we got calls from all the media outlets, and we went and sat down to report it, scared to death... you have no idea how scared we were. But we went anyway. Then he was the one who gathered the same media outlets and gave his statement, his right of reply, and he spoke saying that we were a marginalized population, which we were, it's true, but that we should be detained with thieves, criminals, and murderers, but that we were a bunch of masked people with AIDS who had no place on the streets or anywhere else. This led to the media reporting the incident to the head of security, Norberto Rozua, who had him removed from his public statements. For us, it was a huge achievement that a police chief with so much power over us was dismissed.*

The word community constantly emerges in Karla and Caro's stories. The community is first a form of support and coordination of efforts, and then becomes a political structure. They also think of the archive as a community project, given the need not only to vindicate the past, but also to pass on a legacy to the new generations. Carolina says: "*I think what we are doing is an incredible experience because we are giving information to the new trans generations, because they need to know where we come from, the things that happened before them. Luckily for the girls of today, who already have everything, they have the gender identity law, the equal marriage law, the laws that protect them... that's right, they need to know about the past.*"

*Untangling genealogies*

Although at first glance, violence against travestis and trans people has many points in common with that experienced by other groups, there is a specificity to these experiences that the archive makes explicit. Trans archives not only are testimonies to the painful circumstances of our disappearance, exile, and death, they are also testimony to the unceasing vitality of a collective construction. These archives also document an accomplice society that sustained the patterns of discrimination and abuse throughout periods of time that fall outside the usual chronology of Argentine political history. Malva Solis said that she and her fellow prisoners in Devoto did not realize when it was the dictatorship, because for them it was always the same violence.

Without wishing to enter into the debate about the number of LGBT victims during the dictatorship or insist on discussing whether the military applied specific measures against sexual dissidents, I believe it is important to consider the limitations of thinking about our history using chronologies and analytical tools developed for other cases.

It is becoming increasingly difficult to prove that violence against travestis had any connection with the violence against political dissidents carried out by Peronism with the Triple A (Anticomunist Alliance of Argentina) and the military forces during the last dictatorship. Nor are our experiences comparable to the extermination of Jewish homosexuals during the Holocaust. Curiously, these two milestones in Argentine and universal history are intertwined in Jauregui's account, who claimed to have heard from Marshall Meyer the theory that nearly 400 of those who disappeared during the dictatorship had suffered special mistreatment because of their sexual orientation. But with the increasingly exhaustive review of the narratives of sexual dissidents and victims of the dictatorship, the political operation of linking one genealogy to another becomes absurd and even counterproductive. It does not do justice to the disappeared, whose political struggle was central to their lives, nor does it honor the truth of the travestis, queers, and lesbians who have experienced more extensive violence, more deeply entrenched in the police and more crudely covered up by civil society and the political class.

No mother went out to the square to look for the travestis. The travestis were not given justice. We did not have CONADEP, we did not have *Nunca Más*. We were only armed with fury and friendship to resist the most extreme violence before and after the last dictatorship. Our captors were not an exceptional repressive apparatus, but rather the provincial and national police forces that in many places still patrol the streets. Our whistleblowers were ordinary neighbors who, encouraged by their Christian morals and patriarchal values, snitched on travestis and took advantage of them. Above all, violence against travestis is not a thing of the past. It is a present-day reality. There are still many trans women who live crammed into boarding houses, suffering real estate abuse. Many pay bribes to the police today. Many continue to be punished for the legitimate practice of sex work.

We need our own chronologies because we have always lived on the margins of history. We struggle to construct our own travesti theory because we are an identity that defies the categorizations invented to name us. We create archives and trenches because we want to keep our dead alive. It's not all about political alliances and coalitions; we're not just fighting for legal recognition. We are repairing our community and healing our present so that younger women can imagine a future independent of the challenges of the political will of the moment. We see ourselves in the faces of our mothers and grandmothers of Plaza de Mayo and feel that struggle as our own, because we are the mothers and grandmothers of our own community. In that patchwork of photographs and anecdotes that are our archives, what remains is the desire to embrace those who are absent. As Laly Rolón says with a smile swollen with pride: *"A kiss to the sky for all our friends who are no longer with us. We continue to carry them in our hearts"*

# Never Going Back to Jail: A Travesti Trans Perspective on the Last Military Dictatorship in Argentina

Over the last decade, a series of debates surrounding memory have arisen within the LGBT community in Argentina. Although questions about the effects of democracy on the sexual freedom of gays and lesbians arose almost simultaneously with the restoration of democracy in 1983, new questions and concerns about the repressive strategies used by the state against trans and queer people are currently being revisited. Many political actions are increasingly concerned with historical memory as a fundamental part of the human rights struggle. Among these actions, the Argentine travesti and trans community is deploying specific strategies, such as the creation of memory archives, the dissemination of stories about violence before and after the dictatorship, and demonstrations calling for pensions to repair the institutional violence suffered in the past.

In this article, I will revisit some of these actions for memory carried out by the travesti and trans community in Argentina, in order to recognize how they intersect with the narratives about the dictatorship produced by human rights organizations. I propose to reflect on the tensions that the trans perspective introduces into an intellectual field largely dominated by cis-heterosexual people. I will seek in particular to answer two central questions: What meanings are called into question when we re-discuss the number and status of the victims of the dictatorship? Is it possible to redefine the boundaries between democracy and dictatorship based on the experiences of travestis and transsexuals?

*Historical Background of the LGBT Claim Regarding Victims of the Dictatorship*

According to Rapisardi and Modarelli (2001), the gay and lesbian community suffered persecution during the military dictatorship, but also during the democratic governments that preceded and followed it. This persecution was particularly evident in the community's meeting and leisure places, such as dance clubs, bars, and private parties. Homosexuality was also repressed in public restrooms, as it was believed that these spaces were not only frequented by homosexual men, but also by heterosexual men seeking sexual relief, whom they intended to deceive and seduce. During the government of Juan Carlos Ongania, Police Chief Luis Margaride was responsible for closing public restrooms in train stations and conducting raids on motels and discos as part of the military government's moral crusade against homosexuality and libidinous sexual behavior in general.

This kind of persecution was not exclusive during military governments, but rather a constant in Argentina, at least from 1930 onwards. Although there were no laws that openly punished homosexual behavior, there were some police ordinances that established as suspects any men who were accompanied by underage boys in public places. Accusations of pederasty were also common practice among the morality divisions of the police, who recorded in their files all the "known pederasts" in the city who were accused of various characteristics: effeminate behavior, being in the company of underage boys, wearing clothing inappropriate for males, offering sex in public places, etc. The existence of documents recording this kind of police practice attests to the consolidation of a practice focused on the disciplining of sexuality and social hygiene. During the early years of the Peronist government, Perón even spoke out in favor of establishing brothels in the vicinity of military regiments to prevent cadets and officers from being seduced by homosexual practices (Simonetto, 2020).

Shortly after Raúl Alfonsín's democratic government took office, nascent gay and lesbian groups gathered around the question: Is this what democracy looks like? This provocative slogan challenged the scope of the new democratic state among homosexuals. In April 1984, the Argentine Homosexual Community (CHA) was formed at the Contramano nightclub. One of the CHA's main slogans was the fight against discrimination suffered by the community, especially in the workplace and meeting places. Between December 1983 and March 1984, just three months, an incredible amount of 21,342 people were arrested for background checks. (Bellucci, 2020) The police carried out raids on gay clubs and bars and threatened those arrested with informing their employers or families about their sexuality. In this way, they discouraged gatherings, meetings, and, ultimately, organization. The CHA also participated in the ceremony following the creation of the National Commission on the Disappearance of Persons (CONADEP) with a column of 100 people carrying the organization's flag. Although the CHA understood that it was necessary to seek justice for detained and disappeared gay people, its main vindication about dictatorship's time was to denounce that most of the repressive power of the dictatorship remained in place and persecuted the homosexual community in particular. Even though there were known cases of gay people persecuted by the dictatorship, such as Néstor Perlongher, this persecution was not understood as an exceptional situation, but rather as part of the matrix of violence that constantly threatened the gay community. For this reason, gay activism efforts focused on denouncing the continuity of violence, rather than demanding justice for the victims of the last military dictatorship.

Among the trans community, the demands had other characteristics. Although trans activism as such did not take the form of formal organizations until 1994, there were some previous experiences. In 1986, the first public demonstration by travestis took place in the Plaza de Mayo. This first demonstration led to the formation of a very precarious assembly-based organization called the Travesti's Front. The Travesti's Front organized two demonstrations in Plaza de Mayo, on December 21 and 28, demanding to be received by the Minister of the Interior, Antonio Troccoli, and to deliver a petition. The struggle of the Travesti's Front was aimed at ending the persecution of travesti sex workers on the Pan-American Highway, but also at ending discrimination and social stigma. Although they did not articulate their demands around the issue of the dictatorship, they did use references to human rights discourse to demand a dignified life. In their statements to the press, some declared that they had voted for Alfonsín and felt disappointed by the few changes made in relation to the times of the military dictatorship. On the other hand, in 1991, the public appearance of Karina Urbina and the formation of TRANSDEVI (Transsexuals for the Right to

Life and Identity) brought a totally new rhetoric to the trans political scene. Karina Urbina was the first trans person to seek collaboration with human rights organizations and to construct her narrative of the right to identity in line with the demands of the victims of the dictatorship. Urbina approached organizations such as Abuelas de Plaza de Mayo, the Permanent Assembly for Human Rights, the Delegation of Israeli Associations of Argentina, and the Service, Peace, and Justice Foundation, chaired by Nobel Prize winner Adolfo Pérez Esquivel. She was also the first transsexual person to denounce the exile of many transsexual women and travestis who fled the Argentine military dictatorship and took refuge in Europe. However, Karina Urbina's complaints did not prosper among the hegemonic narratives of LGBT activism, which focused on the voices of travestis and dismissed the voices of transsexual women.

*Transgender Archives and Memory Practices*

Over the last decade, projects have been established to preserve the memory of the travesti and trans community in Argentina, which inevitably address the issue of violence during the military dictatorship. The lack of written documents that give an account of the lives of travestis and transsexuals has mobilized organizations to produce oral records, transcripts, audiovisual recordings, and photographic records about the memories of the travesti/ and trans community. Prior to the creation of archives, there were scattered efforts to collect stories in the voices of trans people themselves, such as the magazine El Teje, which collected life stories written by long-lived travestis, among them the most renowned was Malva Solis. Malva also wrote her own memoirs, which allow us to reconstruct some of the history of the persecution of travestis from 1950 to 1980. Some documentaries, such as Juan Tahuil's "T," Carina Sama's "*Con nombre de Flor*," Cecilia Estalles' "*De la misma especie*," etc., recount the search for a trans memory produced by the community (Butierrez and Simonetto 2021).

These memory projects have reopened debates about the nature of the violence suffered by travestis and trans people during the dictatorship and democracy. These projects reflect trans activism's awareness about the past, but also the need to produce a historical narrative that allows new political demands. In 2017, Marlene Wayar promoted the presentation of a bill under the slogan "To Recognize Is to Repair," which seeks pensions for travestis who were victims of state violence. In the province of Santa Fe, an amendment to the laws on reparations for victims of the military dictatorship enabled twenty travestis victims of the last dictatorship to obtain a life pension to compensate them financially for the violence they suffered when they were detained. Reparation policies, as lifetime pensions, and memory archives have grown together, like two sides of a political strategy that seeks financial reparations on the one hand and the reconstruction of the life stories of travestis and transsexuals on the other.

In 2018, the Trans Memory Archive (TMA) was officially launched, a trans archive and memory project built around the documentary collections that Maria Belen Correa inherited from Claudia Pia Baudracco. Both were key activists in the 1990s, so bringing their documentary collections together allows us to outline the trans scene of the time. These collections were joined by others from travestis who lived in the 1980s and the documentary collection of Malva Solis, which allows us to outline some stories of the trans community from 1950 to the present through old pictures and portraits. In parallel to the creation of the TMA, other trans memory archives emerged in various provinces: the LGBT memory archive of the Province of Salta, the Travesti Trans Memory Archive of the Province of Santa Fe, the LGBT Archive of Santiago del Estero, etc. Each of these archives used different strategies to build their collections. Although most trans archives mainly collect photographs, some have incorporated oral history recordings, audiovisual productions, workshops, and activities.

Alongside the archives promoted by the travesti and trans community, there are other archival and memory projects produced by academic and institutional spaces. For example, CeDINCI's sex-dissident memory project 'Sex and Revolution' explores various topics that allow for the reconstruction of the trans community's memories through letters, notes, and press clippings. The Editorial Sarmiento Documentary Collection (Crónica Newspaper), housed in the Mariano Moreno National Library, has also been reviewed from a transfeminist perspective, resulting in a catalog on "sexual identities" where travestis and transsexuals are one of the main topics. Finally, during 2020 and 2021, the Moléculas Malucas and Archivos Desviados projects have produced a series of studies on sexual dissidence in Argentina that are key to reconstructing the trans history of the region.

*Pan-American Highway: An Open-Sky Clandestine Center*

As part of these research projects that seek to reconstruct the history of the trans and travesti community, a project to record oral histories was recently developed at the National Memory Archive (NMA). The NMA is a key archive in the search for justice for victims of the military dictatorship. During 2018 and 2019, they carried out the recording of oral histories of some LGBT activists who were key in the formation of the first organizations. This documentary collection gathers information focused especially on activism in the 1990s. Recently, as part of a joint project between the NMA and the LGBTIQ+ Area of the Haroldo Conti Cultural Center, a project was developed to recover the oral memories of the travesti sex workers of Pan-American Highway, of whom only press clippings and a few isolated testimonies existed until now. As part of this project, in which I participated by guiding the CC Conti team, six travestis who participated in the Pan-American Highway experience, directly or indirectly at different times, were interviewed. They were: Fabiana Gutierrez, Nadia Natalí Saavedra, Julieta González, Andreína Di Brito, Ivana Tintilay, and Perica Burrometo. The testimonies were recorded on video and are stored at the NMA. The interviews were unstructured, but based on a set of questions that sought to explore various topics: childhood, internal migration, contact with sex work, arrests, violence, access to health care, relationships with neighbors, spaces for organization, mutual support and political demands, exile, and opinions about the current trans context.

Pan-American Highway was the first red-light district visibly identified with travestis. Obviously, before 1983, travestis were engaged in sex work, but they shared red-light districts with cis sex workers. Furthermore, the general public was unaware of the existence of travesti sex workers. For this reason, Pan-American Highway was a watershed moment in the history of travesti identity in Argentina due to its importance in making visible a new sexual experience that until then had been considered restricted solely to the theatrical scene. As Ana Alvarez points out, during the 1970s, travestis were strongly linked to burlesque theater, variety shows, and vaudeville (Álvarez 2022). The presence in 1962 of the famous French transsexual vedette Jacqueline Deufresnoy, better known as *Coccinelle*, opened up a world of possibilities for queers of the time. Coccinelle's influence was huge in South America, inspiring several transsexuals to undergo 'sex change' surgery, but also offering many queers the illusion of being able to express their sexual identity through theatrical performance. In 1971, the debut of the Brazilian travesti company 'Les Girls' inaugurated the popular use of the word travesti to describe the experience of those who dressed as women on stage (Cytryn 2021). On the back of a photograph of the artistic ensemble 'Les Girls,' its director Susy Parker describes the group as a *"group of men in women's clothing in the game called travesti"*. Thus, during the 1970s, this term became popular to describe a theatrical experience in which queers took part. The growing repression of the military dictatorship beginning in 1976 caused the travesti theater phenomenon to retreat, reducing it to small shows in cabarets and brothels.

The travestis of the Pan-AmericanHighway were not a spontaneous and sudden phenomenon. There were already various places where travestis offered sex, from cabarets and brothels located on the outskirts of Buenos Aires to street prostitution. According to Perica Burrometo's testimony (National Memory Archive, 2023), when he arrived in Buenos Aires in 1960, he found small groups of travestis dressed as women offering sex on the streets around the Antonio Lacroze train station. She also recounts the existence of a red-light district on the border between Ciudadela and the Federal Capital. The outskirts of Buenos Aires, the intersections of main roads and highways, and the vicinity of train stations were the places chosen for cruising and the sexual services offered by queers and travestis. Before the consolidation of Pan-American Highway, there were several red-light zones where sex was offered, located on the northern section of Av. del Libertador. Julieta González, a.k.a 'La Trachyn,' recounts that as a young girl she worked with her friends El Negro[14] Miguel and Judith in the Libertador Avenue. At that time, there were not so many travestis in the area, and they offered their sexual services in the San Isidro neighborhood. Perica worked further north in the Beccar area. There are some indications in the press of arrests in the areas of Martinez, Florida, and Olivos (ESTO magazine, September 11, 1987). Work in the Libertador area was rather discreet; travestis dressed as women, trying not to attract too much attention from the police and the military. Clients often mistook travestis for cis women, and they invented various strategies to avoid vaginal intercourse.

Argentina's return to democracy sparked a sentiment of political, cultural, and sexual freedom. Beginning in 1983, and especially during 1984 and 1985, Argentina experienced a democratic spring in which the sensation of sexual and cultural freedom that had existed prior to the dictatorship was restored. This phenomenon was characterized as the unveiling [el destape]. Although it began as a period of open

---

[14] In Argentina, it is quite common to use 'negro' as a nickname. Although it is mostly used to refer to people of colour or those with an indigenous background, it does not have any negative connotations.

dialogue about the crimes of the dictatorship, censorship, and political violence, it quickly spread to the worlds of art, culture, and sexuality. The destape phenomenon had a strong impact on Argentine society's perceptions of the regimes of visibility of the

body and sexuality (Milanesio 2019). However, as Valeria Manzano points out, this openness in the media and cinema with regard to sexuality did not translate into state action in relation to certain sexual minorities (Manzano 2019). As stated in previous works, the destape period meant an expansion in the regime of visibility of travestis in relation to the years of the dictatorship, but police violence, discriminatory acts, and aggression increased during the democratic opening in relation to what travestis had experienced under the military regime.

The Pan-American Highway experience was made possible largely thanks to the climate of cultural and sexual openness during the destape. During the Pan-American Highway period, travestis became an imaginable, albeit clandestine, object of desire. That erotic fantasy surrounding the hyper-feminized bodies of the travesti stars became a real possibility. The Pan-American Highway functioned as a stage where the artists were within reach and could fulfill the most forbidden fantasies. Travestis no longer had to wait for carnival to parade and show off in front of men; the highway offered a permanent carnival atmosphere where sex work took on a new character. Whereas before Pan-American Highway travestis had to dress discreetly to disguise themselves as cis women, from 1983 onwards the areas where travestis worked were almost as spectacular as a theater billboard. Travestis began to work almost naked, displaying their curvy bodies and acting provocatively in front of clients. The combination of exhibitionism and repression caused travestis to move closer to the Pan-American Highway, which at that time was a wasteland surrounded by factories and warehouses. There, the travestis found an ideal space to display themselves almost naked, be accessible to customers who picked them up in their cars, and avoid (though sometimes unsuccessfully) persecution by the police.

The oral histories of the travestis of Pan-American Highway mention that one of the first to learn about the placement of liquid silicone was Negro Miguel. Negro had traveled to Brazil during his vacation and there he learned from Brazilian travestis about silicone injections. Upon his return, Negro agreed to inject silicone into Gina, and after experimenting and perfecting the technique, he became the leading silicone injector in the Tigre area (Testimony of Julieta González. National Memory Archive, 2023). The procedure for injecting silicone was brutal: using veterinary syringes and without anesthesia, silicone was injected into the chest, buttocks, and hips to achieve the effect of a monumental silhouette, smooth skin, and firm, feminine breasts (Kulick 1998). Some began to use silicone on their faces to counteract masculine features and lift their cheekbones. This is how the exuberant bodies of the Pan-American Highway travestis were constructed, forged in the image and likeness of the great Argentine vedettes who flooded cinema screens in the sexy comedies of Olmedo and Porcel. The press echoed the silicone-enhanced bodies of Pan-American Highway, exploiting the morbid fascination with these new sexual technologies, whether in entertainment articles where the travesti stars stripped naked or in the crime pages where the dismembered bodies of dead women were photographed on the side of the road.

The travestis' testimonies of the Pan-American Highway period allow us to clearly problematize the boundaries between dictatorship and democracy. Although certain activist circles seem to believe that trans and queer people were also targets of violence during the last military dictatorship, the accounts of the Pan-American Highway travestis complicate this notion. It does not invalidate the existence of persecution during the dictatorship, as Julieta Gonzalez and Fabiana Gutierrez claim to have been victims of violence during the dictatorship and to have been detained in the clandestine detention center *"Pozo de Banfield,"* but they also suggest that violence continued and even intensified with the advent of democracy. There are also expressions in the travesti memories that question the violence during the dictatorship, for example in the testimony of Perica Burrometo, who asserts that it was during democracy that they suffered the most violence, while the dictatorship was mainly focused on persecuting political adversaries, and there were even military governments where travestis were accepted as part of the artistic and cultural world of Buenos Aires. The testimonies collected in this project allow us to relativize the conclusions reached by previous research, proposing a new chronology for thinking about violence against travestis and transsexuals that begins long before the military governments and extends almost to the early years of the 21st century.

*Rewriting the History of Violence Against Travestis and Transsexuals*

Can the history of the losers be organized using the same chronologies and categories as the winners? Can we write a history of the margins of the state using the times and tools of the historiographical canon? Can the bodies of survivors be the place where the living testimony of violence is archived? The stories and archives that bear witness to the crimes committed against travestis and transsexuals go beyond the limits with which the timelines of conventional historiography are constructed. They flood the political languages legitimized by the state and render them insufficient, permeating them with new and provocative languages that do not understand the boundaries between dictatorships and democracies. Throughout this text, I have presented testimonies and situations that attempt to tell the story of a specific type of violence, orchestrated and carried out with weapons that contradict the political and partisan languages used to narrate Argentine history. Just as cis women's movements once demanded to be made visible in history, today it is urgent to denounce that the history of school textbooks and that promoted by institutions is a cis-centered narrative that speaks of moments and debates that never mattered to the most degraded bodies of civic life.

This text aims to dismantle representations of history that have emerged from a perspective of sexuality studies dominated by cisgender men and women, and constructed with methodological tools that, although useful for thinking about some gay and lesbian trajectories, are not useful for understanding the experiences of travestis and transsexuals. There is a mode of representation of time and space that ignores trans, Black, and poor embodiments, in which the only form of state presence has been surveillance and punishment. Although attempts have been made to discursively link anti-LGBT violence to periods of dictatorship, especially as a political strategy to demand economic reparations, the academic space of trans studies in Latin America must prepare itself for the task of thinking about new chronologies and geographies that represent time and history from the perspective of travestis and transsexuals, even if this runs counter to the discourses of activism.

Although the central proposal of this text is to blur the line between dictatorship and democracy in the case of violence against travestis and transsexuals, it is not a matter of simplifying the issue by pointing out that they suffered the same in both periods. Such a generalization is useless in analytical terms. The aim is to break down the particularities of each period in order to characterize their specificities, while highlighting the common practices and underlying connections between a violence that is not marked by political ideologies, but rather by social ideas about gender and sexual morality. It is even a matter of analyzing and highlighting how post-dictatorship sexual openness allowed for moments of reflection on the diversity of sexual orientations, but not on experiences where the perception of one's own gender was the subject of dispute. The body was the territory of the most crude and disciplining violence of those who understood that travestis and transsexuals were abject, deranged, and pathogenic subjects who should be punished, isolated, and eliminated.

The perspective of trans studies allows us to make this effort to change the focus on sexual orientation from the incarnations of gender, in order to generate new interpretations in which bodies are involved as analytical objects and testimonies. It is the bodies of travestis and transsexuals who have survived dictatorships and democracies that speak of the continuities and disruptions that each experience has had. In this adventurous text, I have tried to reflect a way of thinking about censorship, prohibitions, persecution, punishment, and deprivation from the perspective of those trans bodies that challenged all the moral and visual regimes of the second half of the 20th century in our region. A history of that travesti and transgender flesh, of the rudimentary and furtive technologies that were imprinted on it, of the violence that bruised it and the social discourses that disciplined it, is only the beginning of a history of bodies left on the margins of Argentina's great political history. We owe travestis and transsexuals not only a historical reparation that addresses the urgency of the present, but also a historiographical reparation that gives due weight to the significance of their memories.

Deborah Singer during a
show in 1988

Argentine Travestis Association in a
demonstration against the Police, 1995

Karina Urbina in a demonstration, 1992

Monica Ramos and Perica Burrometo during a funeral, 1987

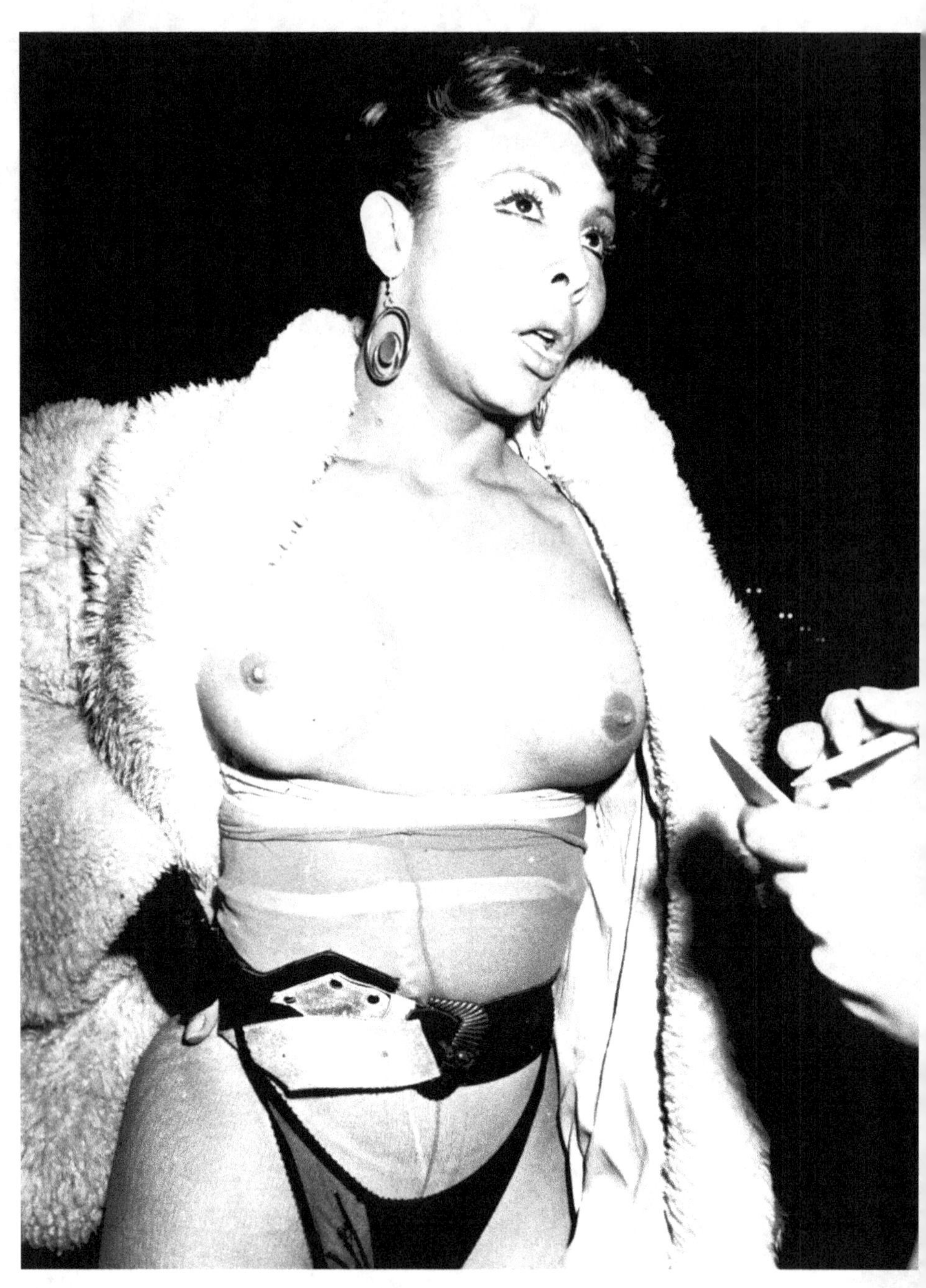

Travesti in Panamerican Highway

Gina, travesti injured in
Panamerican Highway, 1987

Travesti Funeral, 1987

Travesti detained during a party, 1988

Travesti detained and portrayed by the police, 1988

# Transcestors: Genealogies and Biographies

# One is born a woman: Karina Urbina and transsexual activism in the 1990s

Karina Urbina's deep black eyes become crystal clear and shiny in the television close-up. Almost on the verge of tears, Karina tells thousands of talk show viewers the intimate details of her sexuality. With a trembling voice and a crystal clear, broken gaze, Karina manages to say with complete clarity: "I *am a woman, I feel that I am. But unfortunately, I have male genitals.*" The conversation oscillates between Karina's nervousness and the arrogance of a host eager for sensationalism and ratings. Television in the 1990s enjoyed stories about transsexuals and travestis. Entertainment, celebrity-focused talk shows and news featured many travestis and transsexuals who used different strategies to demand recognition and rights. While the travestis acted rude and provocative, filling the screen with scandal, the transsexuals broke down in tears, showing the expected fragility of femininity. It was not just a convincing performance for the cameras; transsexuals demanded in different spaces and in different ways to be recognized as women. Among them, Karina Urbina was a pioneer and a powerful voice who built alliances and brought to public attention the difficulties experienced by those ghost identities, subjected to apartheid by the state.

The first half of the 1990s were decisive years for travesti and transsexual activism in Argentina. From 1992 to 1996 main organizations were formed, slogans and strategies were discussed, and their leaders and political references were outlined. Attempts to reconstruct these processes have focused primarily on the demonstrations carried out by militant groups and have neglected other forms of political agency sustained by individuals in contexts distant from political mainstream narratives. The media presence of some travestis on TV screens was presented by Lohana Berkins as *"a shift in the concealment that had existed until then of travestis as subjects,"* but she pointed out that this exhibitionism did not have *"the challenging character that would later be attributed to it."* The narratives produced at the intersection of activism and academia have privileged the work of formal organizations and have adopted 'trans people' as the central subject of their narratives, it means, the undifferentiated set of expressions of transness that fit within this umbrella concept coined by northern queer theory.

In Second Skins, Jay Prosser criticizes the way in which the category trans unifies a diversity of experiences and establishes, almost as a duty, a non-conforming attitude about gender binarism. Queer theory's political commitment to breaking away from categories that emerged from medical discourse, such as transsexuality, renders invisible the experiences of those who identify as transsexual and choose to live their lives according to socially available norms of femininity and masculinity. Prosser offers an alternative perspective, placing the narratives of transsexual individuals at the forefront and basing them on their own experiences rather than theoretical and political frameworks (Prosser 1998). This perspective is useful for addressing the study of activism in Argentina during the 1990s, where there were clear differences between the demands and claims of two groups identified with different categories: transsexuals and travestis. Although these categories later converged in common political strategies, in the early 1990s they presented themselves very differently and openly debated their positions in various public forums. For the purposes of this work, I consider it extremely important to respect the categories and ways of naming one's own experience expressed in the documents that attest to the political actions of transsexual individuals and organizations. Similarly, I do not intend to analyze their strategies using current political standards, but rather to understand them in the context in which they occurred and over the light of the narratives that were socially available at that time.

Karina Urbina was the first of a generation of transsexual activists who, motivated by different reasons, fought in the courts, on the streets, and in the media for her right to be recognized as a woman. Her demands permeated and transformed these three spaces, long-term building the groundwork for other significant achievements in trans activism, such as the Gender Identity Law passed in 2012.

*"Rectify This Truly Unfair Situation"*

On March 25, 1982, Karina Urbina filed a lawsuit requesting that her female identity be recognized on her ID. Some of the arguments expressed in that ruling have significant and far-reaching importance in the struggle of the travesti and transgender community for the right to identity and bodily self-determination. In the midst of our country's bloodiest military dictatorship and just days before the escalation of war in the Malvinas Islands, Karina Urbina brought her voice to the court: she demanded to be recognized as a woman by the Argentine government. The case passed through various judicial jurisdictions until it reached the

Supreme Court of Justice in December 1989. Although the legal deadlines for filing the complaint had expired, the judges considered that "*it was a good opportunity to set a precedent*" in this issue (Página/12, Mayo 1992). The lawsuit filed by Karina Urbina sparked debate among the judges.

The Supreme Court did not rule on the merits of the case because it considered that the legal deadlines for filing had expired, but some of the statements made by the judges were significant. In a lengthy opinion expressing his dissent, Judge Carlos Fayt refers to the petitioner consistently in with feminine pronouns and considers that Karina's claim does not fall within the scope of a dispute between sectors where the shortcomings generate rights in favor of one and to the detriment of the other. "*If we want to find a plaintiff here, it would be none other than society as a whole, whose sole interest is that of the law,*" said Fayt. For his part, Dr. Mario Calatayud, who voted in favor of the plaintiff's request, stated:

> "*I cannot help but notice the surprise that a decision of this kind may cause to the average morality of our society, but nevertheless I believe it is fair to provide legal protection to that group of individuals known as transsexuals. That is, to those who have managed, through surgery, to align their morphological sex with their psychological sex, voluntarily assuming the risks of that surgery and knowing that they are placing themselves in an irreversible and permanent situation*" (El Cronista Comercial, 14 de Mayo de 1992)

In his statement, Calatayud insists on the free and voluntary choice of this new 'status' for transsexuals and the need for legal recognition and assistance to integrate them into society. He points out that if a favorable ruling is not issued in this regard, they would be marginalized from society and the workplace, and prevented from carrying out the various bureaucratic procedures that require the presentation of IDs cards. "It is *up to the judges to remedy this truly unfair situation, given the absence of any legal provision that addresses this case,*" the judge emphasized.

The legal debate surrounding transsexual issues in Argentina dates back to the 1960s, when Dr. Francisco Defazio gained public notoriety in the press after performing 'sex change' surgeries on several patients. One of them, Maria Vega, went to court to request the rectification of her documents and, contrary to expectations, was arrested. Proceedings were brought against Defazio and his medical team for "*the crime of grievous bodily harm, emasculating a homosexual individual, even though he had requested surgery, without there being a medical condition that required such an operation*" (F.D [*Francisco Defazio*] July 1966). This precedent against Defazio meant that in 1967, during the government of Juan Carlos Ongania, the Medical Practices Act was amended to ban any kind of surgical intervention on the genitals and reproductive organs without prior judicial authorization. These amendments, together with the provisions of Article 89 of the Penal Code and Article 19, paragraph 4, of the Code of Ethics of the Argentine Medical Confederation, were used for several decades to deny trans people access to surgical procedures and medical care.

Finally, in 1969, Dr. Defazio was acquitted of the charges in a ruling that affirmed the patient's right to free disposal of their body and the preeminence of medical knowledge:

*"The removal of male sexual organs and the implantation of*

*a neovagina in an individual who has a feminine intimate psychology and whose body has been treated with hormones to reinforce their sexuality does not constitute the crime of injury when there is doubt in the judge's mind as to the possibility of another more satisfactory solution. The fact that after the operation the individual underwent surgery regularized his nervous system and that all his discomfort, distress, and frustrations disappeared supports the appropriateness of the surgical intervention. The maintenance and restoration of the patient's physical or mental health sometimes requires surgical operations that cause permanent or temporary damage to the patient's body or health, and this in itself does not imply that the surgeon has committed the crime of bodily harm. Consent to mutilating operations has a legal basis, so that the principle of the unavailability of physical integrity gives way to the benefit of health, and punishment is reserved exclusively for cases in which a malicious purpose is pursued. Judges should not interfere in the analysis of disputed medical issues and should exercise extreme caution by avoiding any pronouncement that involves taking a scientific position."* (F.D [Francisco Defazio] December 1966)

These and other legal precedents influenced the position of jurists on the issue of transsexuality. In various communications, conferences, and publications, the debate over whether a transsexual individual who has undergone surgery should be recognized as male or female by the justice system and the state became increasingly prevalent, giving rise to positions that, although dissenting, represented progressive perspectives for their time. In 1996, the recognition of the female identity of transsexual activist Mariela Muñoz opened up the possibility for many travesti and transsexual people to access documents that recorded their self-perceived gender. In 1997, Argentina even allowed the first genital 'adjustment' surgery to be performed on Juana Luffi, a patient diagnosed with *"masculinizing female pseudohermaphroditism."*

*Transsexual People for the Right to Life and Identity*

On the afternoon of May 7, 1991, Karina Urbina led what would be the first public demonstration in defense of the rights of transexual people. With that first act, Transsexuals for the Right to Life and Identity (TRANSDEVI, for the Spanish acronym Transexuales por el Derecho a la Vida y la Identidad) was also born, the first transsexual organization in Argentina. Karina, armed with posters, demonstrated in front of the National Congress in front of the eyes of employees and passersby. That demonstration was the first of nearly a hundred protests in which Karina played a leading role. Sometimes she chained herself to the doors of Congress or held up her characteristic banners denouncing in detail the problems she and her transsexual comrades faced. Sometimes she protested alone, other times accompanied by her mother, friends, and fellow activists such as Carlos Jáuregui. The photos taken of those demonstrations show her stoic and full of conviction in the face of a blind, deaf, and mute government, with which all possible dialogue had been exhausted. These protests took place some time after Karina's lawsuit reached the highest court without any favorable response. Having exhausted all legal options, Karina took action to secure her rights.

These demonstrations were accompanied by other important actions, such as the presentation of bills to amend laws that prevented sexual organ interventions and the rectification of identity documents. Karina Urbina tried to meet with legislators, fully aware that the only way to achieve her demands was to get politicians to enact the changes that the courts had rejected in her particular case. The task was titanic, but Karina never gave up: in 1989, she presented a draft amendment to the laws to the leader of the Peronist Party in the Congress, Alberto Pierri, but never received a response. In 1991, she drafted a bill that would allow for bodily modifications and the recognition of identity and presented it to the then president of the Chamber of Deputies, Eduardo Duhalde, with the support of 62 parliamentarians. This bill also failed to prosper due to the legislators' lack of interest in addressing the issue.

In an interview with Ka-buum Magazine about her reasons for protesting in front of Congress, Karina recounts a story that shares similarities with the experiences of travestis, but also has its own unique aspects:

> "Well, this is how it really is. The police stopped me on the street because I looked "different", so they asked me for my ID. When I gave them my ID card, they took me to the police station. In other words, by arresting me, they violated the Constitution, which states in Article 14 that all people have the right to work and learn. In other words, by arresting me on the street, I no longer have those rights, because if I go to work and the police can detain me for up to 30 days with these police ordinances, then I lose my freedom and my job! From then on, I began to connect with lawyers and judges, and on May 7, I stood alone in front of Congress with signs alluding to sex change. From that date on, I began to connect with other people who had undergone surgery or were still waiting to do so abroad, as well as with other gay,

*lesbian, feminist, and human rights groups in general."*
*(Larson 1994)*

Although transsexuals and travestis were equally affected by the misdemeanor codes that penalized the wearing of clothing of the 'opposite sex' in public and the offering of sex, they chose different paths to deal with this violation of their rights. While travestis fought against the ordinances and demanded their repeal, transsexuals fought to be recognized as women and registered as such in their ID's. For many transsexuals at that time, the experience of sex work was distant, or at least they avoided referring to it as their means of livelihood. Their demands focused on gaining access to the social status of women, being able to raise children, work, study, and participate in public life without their gender being questioned. They did not seek to reaffirm themselves in their own identity category, as travestis did, nor to assert their identity from a distinctive category that questioned the binary, but rather hoped to be able to live like other cis women in society and have access to the same rights. These disputes were expressed in various forums and intensified when the subject of surgical interventions was raised (a topic in which the media had a morbid interest): while some travestis chose not to undergo surgery and lived their identity beyond their genitals, transsexuals presented a clear message to the media, judges, and society: they were born women and feel and experience their gender as such. Living in bodies that do not belong to them is a traumatic situation that they wish to change through surgery and legal provisions that restore their place in society.

However, transsexual activism did not have a segregationist

perspective; on the contrary, it was also pioneering in establishing connections with various feminist, human rights, and gay and lesbian organizations. Karina Urbina's demonstrations in front of Congress were endorsed and celebrated by organizations such as Gays for Civil Rights, the Homosexual Community of Argentina, Grandmothers of Plaza de Mayo, the Permanent Assembly for Human Rights, the Delegation of Israeli Associations of Argentina, and the Service, Peace, and Justice Foundation, chaired by Nobel Prize winner Adolfo Pérez Esquivel. This strategy of creating alliances between different social and political movements set a notable precedent for what would become the activism of travestis and transsexuals in Argentina. Another key aspect of Karina Urbina's activism was TRANSDEVI's active participation in organizing the first Gay and Lesbian Pride Parade in Buenos Aires in 1992. Of the seven organizations participating in that first parade, TRANSDEVI was the only in representation of the trans community. Karina's participation brought new perspectives to the list of demands of the fledgling LGBT movement. Her participation was also imbued with humor, which was captured in a homemade fanzine with personal notes, cartoons and witty jokes about that historic protest, the people who participated in it, and the national political context.

Karina participated in riots against Monsignor Quarracino's statements, during which she was attacked with eggs. Her connection to the gay and lesbian movement in those early years of activism was not only a political strategy, but also a close bond of friendship and complicity. Karina was a regular participant in the meetings and celebrations at the house on 157 Parana St., where Carlos Jauregui lived out his final years. That house was the starting point and meeting place for the actions Karina carried out every week in front of Congress. There, bonds and affections were forged that sustained those joint actions when the movement was still in its first years. It was also the epicenter of disputes and conflicts that eventually provoked Karina's estrangement.

For the second Pride Parade in 1993, TRANSDEVI was no longer among the organizing groups, while organizations such as United Travestis, led by Kenny de Micheli, Sandy Gonzalez, and Gabriela Carrizo, were. Although the alliance between the demands of the gay and lesbian movement and transsexual activism appeared very strong at first, strategic differences between the two sectors began to cause rifts, especially since the emergence and visibility of travestis. It is difficult to understand Karina Urbina's distancing herself from the public scene and activism, but it is easy to understand why gays and lesbians felt closer to travestis and their demands: the misdemeanor codes that penalized travestis for their lifestyle and for engaging in sex work also subjected gays and lesbians to arbitrary arrests and raids. The fight against the police and the ordinances was the strong link between travestis, gays, and lesbians and the platform on which Jáuregui built his activism against discriminatory actions in the city of Buenos Aires in the mid-1990s. Karina points out that the break with Gays DC came after the organization's decision to formally link itself with the Advanced Democracy Front Party, which had Jose Luis Pizzi as its candidate for National Deputy and Carlos Jáuregui as its candidate for city representative[15]. On May 22,

_______________

[15] The list of candidates for the position of deputy in the City of Buenos Aires included Atilio Borón, Noé Jitrik, Inés Izaguirre, Tununa Mercado, José G. Vazeilles, Marcelo Matellanes, Perla Wasserman, Mirta Mántaras, Ernesto Goldar and Alexis Latendorf, among many

1993, Karina resigned from her role as an honorary member of Gays for Civil Rights due to these political differences.

In subsequent years Karina's activism continued for example with her participation in conferences, congresses, demonstrations, and interviews; but her involvement with the rest of the LGBT movement decreased considerably. After her, new figures will emerge within the transsexual movement: Patricia Gauna, Yannina Moreno, Alejandra Costa, and Mariela Muñoz. All of them will continue to fight for recognition as women and the possibility of accessing surgeries in Argentina. Their public appearances will seek to distance themselves as much as possible from travestis, even openly arguing in front of the cameras.

Transsexuals sought to permanently separate themselves from those who saw them as 'men dressed as women' and reaffirmed their identity by performing the role of honest citizens, self-sacrificing mothers, decent professionals, and sensitive and delicate beings. In contrast to the sometimes unruly and scandalous demonstrations that travestis staged on television, transsexuals expressed their feelings of frustration and pain at being deprived of the right to live as "real" women. In their own way, with their own strategy, transsexuals attempted to develop a political voice of their own.

A *Transsexual Voice*

---

other notable figures. José Luis Pizzi, the legal advisor to GaysDC, took the fifth place. This was recorded in the party's founding minutes. The ADF's demands included the demand to "rectify the name and sex in the birth certificate for the full exercise of their civil rights, for trans people and those who have undergone sex reassignment surgery". Extracted from 'Orgullo. Carlos Jáuregui, una biografía política' (2020) by Mabel Bellucci.

Although transsexual activism may seem somewhat conservative, biologistic, and medicalizing in light of current analysis, it is necessary to emphasize the communicative effectiveness of these narratives in the context of the 1990s. These demands were based on the clinical knowledge about sexuality available at that time and seek to promote acceptance in society. They used the imagery of representations of masculinity and femininity to compose a convincing and solid performance for the public. Few scenes are more significant than that of Mariela Muñoz sitting at one of the most famous TV shows, presenting to the entire country the ID card that recognized her as a woman and receiving it from the hands of the ultimate television diva, who reaffirmed her status as an authentic 'lady.' While travestis suffered street persecution and public aggression in front of the cameras, transsexuals composed a friendly image protected by the diagnosis of transsexualism.

However, transsexual activism, and in particular that of Karina Urbina, was the subject of much debate and discussion, but later would be adopted by travesti activists. Karina's discourse often reflects a deeply critical analysis of society. The use of terms such as 'apartheid' to describe the situation of transsexual people in the country reveals the links Karina was able to establish between race, class, and gender. Her intersectional perspective would later be celebrated in the travesti activism of Lohana Berkins, among others. Without wishing to compare clearly different experiences, Karina was very perceptive in her reflections and was able to forge alliances that were sorely needed for travesti and transsexual movements. Much of this was captured in the TRANSDEVI newsletter entitled

The Transsexual Voice.

It is difficult to estimate how many issues of The Transsexual Voice were published and the reach and impact they had. In this article, we can only present a few of them and find some fundamental reflections in their pages. The first issue opens with the following sentence: *"Those who fight against us strengthen our nerves and perfect our skills. Our adversary only helps us,"* which encapsulates a spirit of battle and perseverance very characteristic of Karina's actions[16]. This first issue introduces the people who make up TRANSDEVI and who accompany its actions (anthropologists, lawyers, etc.), a brief genealogy of its three years of activism, and the main points of its political proposal. Subsequent issues feature articles with anti-clerical, anti-fascist, and reflective positions on disabilities, HIV, male transsexuality, and feminism. The magazine contains articles on abortion, criticism of Quarraccino and the power of the Catholic Church, articles on neo-Nazi groups, and many passages where she slips in reflections that go far beyond the strictly transsexual issue. One issue even presents a bill drafted by some members of parliament to demand changes to the anti-discrimination law. This bill has the support of TRANSDEVI and is accompanied by an article written by Urbina for the magazine The Parliamentarian entitled "The Law of Desire." This law is supported because it considers that "it will enable the inclusion of transsexual women and men into a society that is struggling to rid itself of archaic and obscurantist concepts," adding that "transsexual people are undocumented human beings, therefore we ask the

---

[16] This sentence was originally made by Edmund Burke, a writer, philosopher, and politician who is considered the father of British conservative liberalism.

Deputies and Senators to promptly approve the bill (...) so that we are included in its protection as persons with legitimate human, civil, and social rights." The terminology and conceptual clarity are surprising for a publication from 1994. It is also important to note the inclusion of male transsexual experiences into TRANSDEVI, as not only was there reflection on the subject, but one of its active members was a transsexual man.

***

The activism of Karina Urbina and the transsexuals of the nineties constantly reveals porous edges and textures that allow us to understand other types of trajectories and narratives that have been unjustly forgotten. The current urgency to think about history leads us to trace linear and teleological trajectories that crescendo toward the current achievements of the trans movement. We talk about processes as if they were staggered, straight steps leading from the incipient to the glorious, like a machine producing political events in a single direction. But how do we understand the politicity? Where do we draw the line between performance, media, and protest? When do we value certain actions as activism, and why do we leave others in an ancient prehistoric genesis? This article presents only a few fragments of this labyrinth of stories about transsexual women and Karina Urbina, and yet it allows us to see how necessary it is to refine our discourse on when, where, and how travesti and trans movements began to have the power to discuss beyond identity. We need to retrace these paths and lift our veils to see how much our present owes to those comrades who were already mobilizing when there was hardly a movement.

# Jailbirds: The Activism of Pelusa Liendro and Rosario Sansone Against the Police in Salta

On November 6, 2004, Pelusa Liendro and her travesti crew started the first Pride Parade in Salta[17]. The starting line for that unholy procession was the Hernando de Lerma neighborhood, a historic area of cruising and red-light district where every night a battle was fought between Salta's patriarchal morality and the travestis. Those sidewalks were the scene of police harassment, the frowns of scandalized neighbors, and hooded clients seeking pleasure in those sensual bodies.

There were just over thirty travestis, tired of violence and discrimination. They walked down across the streets of the red-light district, passing in front of the same police stations where they were especially mistreated every night. This time they did not get into the patrol car handcuffed; they went with their arms raised and standing, ready to fight. The parade continued towards the city center, ending at the main square, where they demanded the repeal of the misdemeanor codes that criminalized sex work on public streets and transvestism.

They were also afraid. They and their bodies knew that this demonstration would not end without reprisals. A few hours later they would have to return to the streets to earn a living, to pay bribes to the same cops they had just confronted, to deal with aggressive clients and the whispers of the neighborhood. Those feathers, those costumes, those

[17] Salta is a small town located in the northern region of Argentina.

faces covered in glitter, were a way of showing their queer pride and also a sparkling and

brazen camouflage to enter the battlefield and try to emerge unscathed.

Over time, memories of the First Pride Parade in Salta faded, giving way to disputes between groups, personal pettiness, and conflicts between political ideologies. Only the few travestis who accompanied Pelusa in the first demonstrations are able to recall, without photos or videos, the excitement of that first event in which they timidly dared to imagine a group integrated and led by trans women. That epic struggle was about promoting the organization of trans sex workers who, tired of dodging death, wanted to assert their rights as sex workers.

Perhaps at this point it is worth pausing. The history of the travesti movement in Salta is made up of many narratives that have been battling for a place at the center of the stage and producing a margin in which many activist experiences, half written and half erased, have been left behind, sometimes unfairly referred to as 'activism before activism.' Perhaps because they arose suddenly and were fueled by urgency, or because they did not form formal organizations; because their members had no idea what they were doing, but did it anyway; or because their methods mixed carnival and festivity with a harsh cry that challenged the system.

And that is where the whores were left behind. Activism focused more on the right to identity, social inclusion, and the creation of a normalized travesti that was pharmaco-politically adapted to society. Hand in hand with well-meaning feminists, trans organizations began to fight for equal conditions with other women and to demand education, formal jobs, healthcare, and quotas in political representation. These demands are undoubtedly more than valid and correlate with the concrete demands of many trans women who, exhausted of the streets and marginalization, have been projecting domesticated ways of living their lives. The slogans used by the travestis in the streets to demand to work without being persecuted and murdered by the police, the repeal of the ordinances that criminalized them, and the creation of red-light districts where they could engage in sex work, have been watered down.

Pelusa was a sex worker whose activism focused on calling for the repeal of ordinances 114 and 115, which condemned sex work, and demanding the creation of a 'red-light district' where she could work without facing harassment from neighbors and security forces. A newspaper article published in December 2006 remembers her as follows:

> "From her position and based on her convictions, Pelusa wanted to occupy the space that had been taken away from her throughout her life for not conforming to what was 'established' by God and some human beings. Pelusa wanted her peer group to organize to confront the exclusion and lack of work that made them 'subordinates,' less valuable than other people with politically correct bodies, sexualities, and genders."

Pelusa had a well-defined proposal and vision, as opposed to other leaders at that time. Pelusa was convinced that in order to organize, it was necessary to defend the practice of prostitution and demand an end to its persecution, which is why she and her colleagues called for a red-light district.

At her side, her best friend Rosario Sansone also joined this struggle, tired of the abuse and aware of the power of demonstrations in other cities across the country. In the only available account of that first parade, Rosario declared:

> "It's not a protest, it's a party. It's our gay pride party. This parade was first held in New York in 1977 and in Buenos Aires in 1992. This is the first one in Salta. But even though this is a party, we can't forget that in Salta the police beat up travestis. I myself was detained until a few days ago. They deprived me of my liberty for a week and beat me at the 2nd Police Station. They brought five charges against me. And look, I still have the bruises (she pulls up her dress and shows the marks of the physical punishment). The governor Romero tries to hide this, but the attacks against travestis continue. That is why we are organizing an association to defend our rights."

In this same article, a journalist and leading figure in Salta feminism consulted on the matter points out the "lack of political awareness" among the trans community and the absence of a leader for the movement. She concludes by stating that travestis *"when they reach a level of awareness about their situation within society, abandon prostitution and turn to political struggle,"* once again emphasizing this distinction between the struggle for appropriate conditions for sex work and the aspiration for a 'decent' life.

Pelusa and Rosario's struggle was apparently not political enough to be valued at the time, nor was it over the years, as the many efforts made to form that association were solitary, without achieving coordination with gay, lesbian or feminist organizations. However, in 2004, both participated in a panel at the National University of Salta, promoted by some students who were part of a space for reflection on gender and feminism. Although attendance was low, it was a first step in the academic context to problematize sex work, police violence, and transvestism.

In 2005, the Second Pride Parade took place and the number of travestis who joined the protest increased, as did the level of spectacularity in the parade. The parade was originally an event led by travesti sex workers and sustained by their own bodies. They were the first to make themselves visible, to confront state surveillance, to endure the mockery of occasional spectators, and to dare to enter the city downtown with their irreverence, their swaying hips, and their feathers. The city streets started to swarm with a peculiar mix of carnival and protest, bringing with it music, colors, and a degree of scandal and indecency, the latter two offenses, according to the code of misdemeanors, being enough to land the girls in jail for several weeks.

During those years, Pelusa and her friend Rosario became an unavoidable reference for the demands of the travesti community, which is why they were frequently sought out by the media. *"The media are the ones who are helping us. The news, they are the ones who are giving us a hand by showing what really happens to us,"* says Rosario in an interview, while denouncing the neglect of the political class in Salta:

> *"We filed (the complaints) with the Human Rights Minister, with Dr. Guillén, with the public prosecutors on duty... but these are complaints that date back thirteen, fifteen, or sixteen months ago which anyone paid attention to and were forgotten. I told Dr. Guillén from the Human Rights*

These were dark years for the province of Salta, as the security forces enjoyed impunity that allowed them to operate with total impunity and in the most brutal manner. On April 1, 2005, the provincial police, responding to orders from then-Secretary of Security Gustavo Ferraris, used rubber bullets, tear gas, and batons to repress a group of teachers who were on strike and intended to camp out in Plaza 9 de Julio. This event, known as The Night of the Chalk, was one of the most extreme expressions of state violence under Juan Carlos Romero government, but it was not the only one. Social protest had been repressed throughout Juan Carlos Romero's administration, and travestis experienced this violence every weekend when they took to the streets:

"No, nobody feels safe in Salta. There are many girls here (in Buenos Aires) because two years ago there was an operation called 'Red Light District Cleanup.' There were raids every day, continuously, at any time, and you couldn't walk the streets of Salta, so you had to flee the city, the province. And now I came here because the government has launched a new operation, which Gustavo Ferrari, the secretary of security, is publicizing in the media. I don't know if prostitution will continue to exist. If something happens to us, other girls will come, who, unfortunately, are people who are in a situation of prostitution. Maybe we want something else for ourselves, but it hasn't happened. There are many *underage girls on the streets who are working and suffering the same as me. And that's what hurt us. A fifteen- or sixteen-year-old girl being raped, abused, taken to prison, all of that outraged us greatly, and that's why we marched."*

When Rosario says 'our marches,' she is referring not only to the pride parades they had organized together with Pelusa, but also to many demonstrations that took place between 2003 and 2006 to demand the end to police violence, which was the central concern of their colleagues. When they began to organize, their main demand was that the police stop beating them, stop charging them bribes, and stop asking them for "sexual favors." The travestis demanded that at least the regulatory frameworks be complied with and that detentions not exceed four hours, since they pointed out that they often spent days in detention. Many sex workers ended up with criminal charges against them, as charges of contempt, assault, or drug possession were fabricated against them without any evidence.

By 2006, the travestis organized around the charismatic leadership of Pelusa began to demand more than just compliance with the law; they wanted to achieve the repeal of the code of misdemeanors that criminalized the offering of sex in public, scandal, and indecent exposure. This was because Pelusa and her colleagues were becoming more specialized in their role as activists and understood that the legal framework provided by the ordinances offered no guarantees for the sex work. Moreover, the police would continue to have the combined powers of prosecutor, investigator, and judge for crimes covered by that law, which reinforced the arbitrary treatment of travestis. This made it urgent for the legislative branch to begin discussing the modification of several of the ordinances and for the municipality to take precautionary measures in the meantime. Therefore, the girls demanded the establishment of a red-light district far from residential neighborhoods to avoid conflicts with neighbors and ensure they would no longer be subject to police persecution.

These lawsuits gave Pelusa's struggle greater visibility and began to be frequently consulted by the media. They were also the subject of intense surveillance and persecution by the police. It should be remembered that various human rights organizations, journalists, and workers unions had denounced the existence of a 'police information group' known as D2 that operated in the province and monitored social leaders and opposition journalists and reported on various protests, even infiltrating assemblies and private meetings. Rosario stated that *"when my mom heard about the marches, she told me not to go because she was very afraid. But I continued anyway, and so did Pelusa. Both of us."* Everything was about to change in November 2006.

On Tuesday, November 7, 2006, Pelusa led what would be her last pride parade. Twenty-two days later, she would be found dead from seven stab wounds inside her car, after having dedicated the last four years of her life to organizing the travestis of Salta and denouncing the police by all possible ways.

That third Pride Parade was growing in size, no longer limited to a few travestis, but with more than a hundred people taking to the streets, accompanied by some gays and lesbians who were timidly beginning to participate in the event. Some of the few available photographs of Pelusa were taken at that last march, in which she is seen standing with a banner protesting against police abuse and another in which, microphone in hand, alongside the Pride and Argentine flags, she gave what she did not know would be her last speech to her companions. On that occasion, she once again pointed the finger at the police:

*"We are more afraid of the police than of criminals. Criminals want to rob us. But the police do more than that: they take our money, sexually abuse us, don't pay us, and also put us in jail."*

But she also pointed out the responsibility of Juan Carlos Romero's government in the extreme marginalization experienced by travestis:

*"The politicians don't sit down to discuss what's happening to us. They only know the policy of fines and jail. That doesn't solve the problem. We don't want to bother the neighbors in the area where we are. That's why we're asking to be assigned a red-light district, on the side avenue of the City Stadium."*

A couple of weeks later, Pelusa was interviewed by the TV show The Other Side, which was broadcast on a local cable channel and presented the voices of the marginalized sectors of Salta society through investigative journalism. The journalist in charge of the program, Martín Sánchez, knew Pelusa for her work at the forefront of the travesti movement in Salta and had covered demonstrations on other occasions. He met Pelusa, Rosario, and a couple of other girls. They began to tell him about the violence they faced on a daily basis. From there, they drove to the red-light district and at one point a patrol car approached. Pelusa got out of the vehicle and approached the patrol car.

After talking for a while from the passenger window, he handed the officers a bill and returned to the car where Sánchez and a cameraman were recording the sequence. *"Did you see that? He asked me for a bribe,"* said Pelusa, but in the deep darkness of that block, the distance between the camera and the scene, and due to the poor quality available in those years, the videos show nothing incriminating. However, a few minutes later, several patrol cars, trucks, and a large number of policemen from the second police station arrived at the scene.

As a result of the operation, the police arrested Pelusa, Rosario, and the journalists. According to Martín's story, the fact that the press was present during the operation somehow softened the police's treatment of the girls, who were released a few hours later, although he emphasizes that the brutality and magnitude of the operation struck him as remarkable. After those arrests, the girls worked calmly throughout the week, as the Security Secretariat chose to preserve the image of the police, aware of the existence of the footage. But there was already a sense in the air that reprisals would soon follow, according to Rosario:

> *"Well, the show is going to air and Pelu is very worried. I noticed her looking very scared for the first time. We were in her car and she told me that we were taking a big risk, and I told her that nothing was going to happen to us. But I suspected that something was going to happen to us. I suspected that it would only be a beating. And... They killed my friend."*

Pelusa was found stabbed inside her car ten days after the program aired, on a rainy night. At around seven in the evening, her friends had called her to coordinate their outing to the red-light district, to which Rosario replied that she didn't think she would go out that night because it was raining and very cold. Rosario received another call from a mysterious client but decided not to go to the appointment because she didn't want to go out dressed casually. That coquetry may have saved her life. Pelusa also received a mysterious call and a short time later was found inside her car parked in a dark alley. She was seriously injured and was helped by some neighbors who called 911 when they saw her bleeding, but when she arrived at the hospital, she was dead. Pelusa just kept repeating, "*Don't let me die,*" although Rosario understood that in her last words, she pointed to her killers, but the police made sure that this would never be known. A neighbor interviewed by the press said that Pelusa's last words were incomprehensible due to the severity of the wounds to her throat.

As soon as the news broke, thousands of rumors began to circulate, shocking the entire community. The police were quick to present an alibi that criminalized Pelusa's life, as Rosario recounts.

> *"After that, they wanted to link my friend to drugs. That was the first thing they did. We weren't even holding a wake because my friend was still in the morgue. And the police were already in the media saying that Pelusa had been killed over a drug deal. And my friend wasn't involved in that, I'm very sure of that. The police were on our heels 24 hours a day because of our struggle. I couldn't even mourn her in peace because they kept taking me away, the brigades kept coming. Then they told me I was the main suspect. I wanted to die! I saw my friend dead and I saw myself in prison."*

During the early hours of the case, frightened by the

impunity of the police and politicians, Pelusa's family and friends avoided making any big statements. They were overcome with grief and fear. The authorities constantly asked if they knew who Pelusa's enemies might be, but out of fear, no one dared to speak, also to avoid confusion in the face of the many versions that the press had begun to present. But once the funeral was over, Rosario declared, her voice broken with tears, that "*Pelu had a great enemy, a very powerful one: the police.*"

However, the police lead was not thoroughly investigated. Raids were carried out on the channel where the videos that Rosario claimed led to Pelusa's death had been broadcast, and testimonies were taken from journalists, but all of this remained at the preliminary investigation stage and was never revisited. Pelusa's death was surrounded by rumors, some of which were even planted to obstruct the trial, but all of them aimed to tarnish the image of the travesti leader. Pedophilia, drugs, sodomy, extortion, abuse, AIDS; the entire arsenal of heteropatriarchal justice was deployed in the investigation of the case, burying Pelusa's reputation and, with it, her memory ever deeper.

Pelusa's legacy was once again expressed in the streets. Travestis began marching every day to demand an investigation into the police, to denounce their abuses, to remind society that they were not safe, and even less so after the brutal crime against their friend. Those demonstrations prompted the government to sit down for the first time to talk with the victims. A government car pulled up outside Rosario's humble home and told her they had good news for her. "*There is no more good news for me,*" she replied. They invited her to a meeting at the Government House, but she was suspicious and afraid, so her younger sister accompanied her. Pelusa's parents also attended. At that meeting, they came face to face for the first time with the ministers, who announced that they were going to set up a red-light district for travestis and offer a reward for anyone who could provide information about Pelusa's murder, but they asked for something in return:

> "They asked me to stop protesting against the police. Because when people see the police, they feel safe. I told them that's not true, because I'm also a person, and when I see the police, I feel afraid. There's no way I'm putting myself in the hands of the police. Five minutes is enough time for them to do whatever they want to me, or even take my life. They asked me to stop protesting, but I continued marching every month. The first few weeks I marched three times in a row. One march per week. Thank God my colleagues accompanied me despite their fear."

The events surrounding the investigation into Pelusa's murder are not relevant to this article for two reasons. Firstly, because we are motivated by the desire to remember her life, her activism, and the struggles that she and her companions bravely fought before the creation of organizations and state agencies designed to protect the trans community. Secondly, because all the debates and events following her murder only served to revictimize Pelusa and, with her, all the travestis and sex workers of Salta.

The persecution continued, becoming increasingly intense, and Pelusa's murder served as a disciplinary discourse, attempting to restore order through brutality and fear. Many of Pelusa's friends emigrated to Buenos Aires, fearful of becoming the next victims. Those who remained gradually began to abandon the streets or walk them silently. A social representation of travestis as marginalized and criminal individuals involved in crimes became firmly established in Salta's society. For this reason, each of the bodies that appeared was immediately labeled as dangerous and subversive.

The impact of Pelusa's murder also galvanized the LGBT community's organizing efforts. After her death, new associations emerged that took up the baton of organizing Pride Parades. Groups that existed at the national level met in Salta a couple of years later and began to organize and support local initiatives. Pride Parades grew in number and in their demands. The memory of Pelusa remained present, although ideological differences led to two or three marches taking place in parallel and, as a result, different appropriations of the figure of the historic Pelusa. Her fellow sex workers always remembered her and, year after year, carried on her legacy.

In 2013, at the end of the march, a commemorative plaque was presented to the family. Among the crowd, her friends cheered Pelusa's name, shouting for the red-light district and for a single march. Standing on stage, her mother asked that *you always accompany the girls* and that the community unite. *"I know Pelusa is here right now, and I think she must be happy about everything. But she would be even happier if all of you were together in a single parade, as she wanted. Pelusa wanted everyone to be united in a single struggle."*

# Pelusa, Vanesa, and Marcela: Counter-Memories of Sex Work from a Travesti Perspective

> *"We may disagree, we may have ideas that will never convince each other, but we base ourselves on the fact that we all experienced the same violence. Whatever we say, we cannot deny that our realities are the same and that what happens to one of us today will sooner or later happen to me too."* (Lohana Berkins 2001)

In recent years, the emergence of the issue of trans memory has captured the attention of researchers, the media, and the cis audience. The pictures collected in the trans archives evoke that pristine feeling of childhood, when we looked through family albums depicting birthdays and vacations. But trans memory speaks of more than just our daily lives; each image transports our memories to other scenes, like a relentless flashback that takes us through red-light districts, the Pan-American Highway, dungeons, and the meetings and demonstrations where activism began. This incessant flashback is fed back into the interventions made on this archive every time it is exhibited, recounted, and investigated. Every glance that scans it is an operation that produces more memories.

This review will also be a narrative interrupted by flashbacks, jumping back and forth without much order between the personal stories of some travesti activists and reflections on how current political disputes influence the production of trans memory. In particular, I will look at some biographies of travesti women engaged in sex work who have been little discussed, based on a narrative that ignores the categories they chose to identify themselves with and the political demands they upheld during their lives. Why are some victims remembered more than others? How do current debates within the trans movement determine which stories are considered memorable and which are not? What conflicts exist in the dialogue between the past and the activist narratives of the present? These questions will be answered through the stories of Pelusa Liendro, Marcela Chocobar, and Vanesa Ledesma, three travestis engaged in sex work who were murdered and victimized by the justice system, the press, and the police. In addition to this, their memories have been manipulated and forgotten.

*Pelusa Liendro*

When Tatiana Ortíz's body was found in 2001 on the slopes of a hill in Salta, her friends knew she had been murdered. The police used to take them to the hill and abuse them when they refused to pay bribes. Pelusa Liendro had already had enough. With her friend Rosario Sansone, she began to convince the other travestis that they should organize to fight against the police and demand a red-light district where they could work without harassment from neighbors. Their demand for free sex work was the backbone of the travesti and trans movement in Salta. Pelusa was the one who put her body on the line to build this demand. In 2004, Pelusa and Rosario, and other 80 travestis and sex workers, organized the First Pride Parade, which began in the red-light district, then passed by the 2nd Police

Station, where most persecuted travestis, and ended at the Provincial Legislative Building.

After that first parade, some cohesion was finally achieved among the travestis, and the media became aware of their demands and the conditions in which they worked. This notoriety came hand in hand with severe reprimands from the police, but also with bonds of solidarity between this growing movement and some existing feminist spaces. Rosario and Pelusa participated in a panel at the National University of Salta organized by a gender study group promoted by students, gained notoriety in the independent media, and managed to gather more and more support to carry out rallies and demands. In 2005, they organized the Second Pride Parade with an increasing number of participants putting their bodies on the line for a difficult and uncomfortable demand, in the midst of one of the most conservative cities in Argentina.

During 2006, the provincial government, led by Juan Carlos Romero, had granted impunity to the Minister of Security, Gustavo Ferraris, and the entire police leadership. A special unit was established to monitor social leaders and independent journalists, a fact that came to light after a long demonstration by teachers, during which the protest was brutally repressed and its main leaders were threatened and illegally investigated (Prensa Obrera 2007). This systematic surveillance extended to travestis, who had to avoid police checks more frequently, suffered severe beatings, and paid large bribes to be able to work. Several demonstrations calling for the repeal of the codes of misdemeanours had increased, and Pelusa's public exposure was unprecedented. They had often been threatened, but they believed that because of the notoriety of their activism, the police would not dare to do anything to them.

In early November 2006, Pelusa and Rosario organized the third Pride Parade, which was increasingly massive. Some days later, they gave an interview for a television program in which they highlighted the reality of travestis and the sex work, even recording a moment when Pelusa was asked to pay a bribe. The interview culminated in the arrest of the travestis and the journalists accompanying them. A week after the program aired, Pelusa was found dead in her car in a dark street, her throat slit and showing signs of extreme violence (Sansone 2007).

In the interview conducted a few days before his murder, Pelusa succinctly stated the reasons behind her activism:

> My struggle is this: to find an area where all the travestis can be at peace, where we don't bother the neighbors as we do where we are now, because we understand that we are causing a nuisance due to the high demand for our services in Salta. We are in very high demand. So we want to be given an area next to the City Stadium, where we won't bother anyone. Obviously, we don't want a liberated zone; we want an area controlled by the police. Why? Because of the crimes that can occur, such as theft and gangs that come to cause trouble. We want a controlled area, we want the police to protect us… we want to stop being afraid of them. (Sanchez 2007)

Following the news of her murder, countless rumors and theories circulated about the travesti leader. Pelusa was linked to drugs, pedophilia, crime, revenge, and AIDS. Her body was re-victimized by the media, with the complicity of the police and the justice system, who planted false leads adding pages to a court file that is a summary of the violence to which travestis are always exposed. The riots demanding justice did not stop. Frightened, beaten, tired but not defeated, the travestis preferred to take refuge and put off the struggle because without Pelusa it had become hard. Although suspicions pointed to the police having killed Pelusa because of her increasingly irritating activism and as a clear message of intimidation to her followers, that line of investigation was never pursued.

*Vanesa Ledesma*

In the early hours of February 11, 2000, at Bar Mikons in the city of Córdoba, the police arrested Vanesa after accusing her of damaging property during a fight with customers. For the next five days, none of her friends from the United Travestis Association of Córdoba (ATUC, for the Spanish acronym Asociación de Travestis Unidas de Córdoba) heard anything about her. They did not see her working on the streets after she had been taken to the Police Station. On February 16, the police recorded on Vanesa Ledesma's death certificate that she had died of a heart attack, aggravated by the fact that she had congenital malformations, HIV, syphilis, and used drugs. A closed coffin was delivered for their mourners, but at the insistence of the travestis, it was opened to reveal the horrible truth: Vanesa had been beaten, tortured, and her body was covered with scratches, cuts, and marks from being tied up at the wrists. Vanesa Piedrabuena, also an ATUC activist, was able to take a photograph showing the bruised and tortured body of her friend.

The scandalous and extreme lifestyles of travestis used to be (and still are) the perfect excuse for law enforcement to justify persecution. In the province of Córdoba, there were two articles in the code of misdemeanors that penalized travestis. One of them referred to the 'scandal', which was entirely at the discretion of the police officers on duty. Ivanna Aguilera recounts the situation in those years with these words:

*"... In 1990, we founded the first LGBT organization in Córdoba, the Association Against Homosexual Discrimination (ACoDHo, for the Spanish acronym Asociación contra la Discriminación Homosexual). We began to demand our rights, especially the right to move freely, and we began to work on the Misdemeanor Codes of the Province of Córdoba, especially with a legislator. When the Misdemeanor Codes were revised, we managed to repeal Article 19, and although we fought to have Article 22, on 'scandalous prostitution', repealed. We were unable to get it removed. Instead, it was reinterpreted in Article 45bis, which remains in force today and at least provides some more possibilities for defense because there is not as much discretion for its application by the police."* (Aguilera 2020)

Vanesa Ledesma and her friends lived amid scandal. Remaining silent or bowing their heads was not an option when the violence of the police institution was so brutal. The only way to achieve a little justice and be respected was to break everything, to set it on fire. In a short documentary (Monsú & Tortosa 2001), Vanesa Piedrabuena, president of ATUC and friend of Ledesma, recounts the ways in which they rebelled against the police to obtain justice:

*"What you want is trouble again. You want chaos in here again. You're going to get it again, because I'm going to do it*

*again. But I'm not going to go to them anymore, I'm going to go straight in and beat them up with all the crazy women in there, I'm going to smash everything up, I'm going to get out and leave. It's as simple as that, and they know I'm going to do it. I'm not threatening them: I'm telling them, and I'm going to do it."*

The sequence continues with Vanesa and the other trans girls protesting in chains in front of the police and Human Rights Secretary Guillermo Jhonson. Faced with the threat of eviction and repression, Vanesa Piedrabuena defended her companions by threatening to set herself on fire, while holding a bottle of gasoline.

This carefree, scandalous, and aggressive activism established the foundation for travesti activism in Córdoba. After the murder of Vanesa Ledesma, organizations demanded justice and succeeded in getting Public Prosecutor Luis Raúl Ferrando to bring charges against the police officers Pedro López, Carlos Guanca, Julio Quintero, Carlos Ruiz, Claudia Cornejo, Américo Juárez, Gustavo Pérez, and Gustavo Casas, as well as an unidentified officer known only by his nickname Tetris, accusing them of *"abuse in the line of duty."* However, the police, the justice system, and the executive branch in Córdoba covered up the case. It was Piedrabuena activism that prompted hundreds of letters demanding justice to be sent to the offices of then-Governor José De la Sota. Amnesty International named this case as one of six symbolic cases of torture in prisons and institutional violence worldwide due to the repercussions of this case. To date, no police officer has been tried for the murder of Vanesa Ledesma.

*Marcela Chocobar*

Marcela Chocobar was from Salta. Like many people from northwestern Argentina, she had traveled with her sisters to the Patagonian region, a region with more job opportunities due their growing industrial sector. When she arrived in Río Gallegos, she began working in a cabaret run by another older travesti. On her nights off, she would go out dancing with her friends. One of those nights, Marcela did not return. Her sudden absence worried her sisters, they went to look for her at her apartment and found no signs that she had returned. They went to report her missing, but the police told them that their sister must be out partying. Sluts, party girls, and travestis never seem to be the victims, even though they usually are. When they finally entered the apartment, they noticed that one of her cell phones, the one she used with clients, was missing. Days passed and weeks went by, and no one knew what had happened to Marcela. Everyone imagined her out partying, hooking up, drinking too much. A few weeks after her missing, they found her decapitated corpse in a wasteland in the outskirts of the city.

*"Why she got into a car alone at that time of night?,"* people asked Marcela's sister. On that night in September 2015, Marcela left the nightclub, where she had gone dancing with some friends, and little is known about what happened next. Official reports say that two men took her in a car to a cabin with the promise of paying her for sex. But many accounts indicate that Marcela knew Martín Baez, one of the sons of the multimillionaire Kirchnerist businessman Lázaro Baez (Alarcón 2019). In several conversations, Marcela had mentioned that she knew Baez, and her friends had often seen her leave in the middle of a party after receiving a call from a VIP client. It is likely that Marcela got

into that car that night because she knew who was driving it and who they were meeting with. In any case, that truth will remain hidden, like her body, under a web of complicity and corruption. Although the courts convicted two people for her murder, Marcela's sisters are still fighting to find out where her corpse is, what was done with it, and who the real perpetrators of this heinous crime were.

Although many still remember Marcela and hold events and demonstrations every year demanding justice, the crime is ignored beyond the frontiers of Patagonia. Her memory remains distant, like the death of a distant stranger who does not seem to affect us so much. Her life seems frozen in the distant latitudes of the cold Patagonian landscape. And Marcela's life? Very little is said about her dreams, projects, and desires cut short by transvesticide. Memory evokes her only as a victim, as a true crime show. As a body, without a head or face. We are left with the task of constructing the most intimate plot of this story, the network of affections woven behind the crime, the human fiber that fills the file with something more than ink.

### Bad Victims

The stories of Pelusa, Vanesa, and Marcela have aspects that link them and others that highlight their differences. They are separated by a 15-year time span in which the regulatory framework for travestis has changed significantly, especially as a result of the trans activism's struggles. Vanesa's story is similar to that of thousands of other travestis in the 1990s, marked by police persecution and constant punishment based on the use of misdemeanor codes. And although Pelusa's struggle was also against the codes, for Marcela that path has been smoothed, and she even had the right to gender identity. But the similarities between these crimes, so distant in time, draw attention to how vague our understanding of the success of some public policies can be. These stories also reveal how experiences outside the metropolitan bubble often skew our perception of the dimensions and chronology of trans activism, showing us a range of experiences distant in space.

Despite these differences, what unites the experiences of Pelusa, Vanesa, and Marcela is the sex work, the street, the night, and the way in which they navigated the boundaries of morality, decency, and bourgeois order with the arrogance of their lives. The stories often told about them attempt to portray their lives as victims of an adverse context caused by the segregation of the trans community through institutional violence and the absence of policies. But whether this was the case or not, they embraced their scandalous lifestyles. Their untamed lives condemned them post-mortem to silent oblivion. Their lives were viewed with suspicion, and that is why their deaths resonate differently, even for activists. Their lives and murders are not the pristine portrait of travesti activists who were victims of political persecution; they are not good citizens marked by a twist of fate; they are not passive victims of a context that crushes their will. They are bad victims.

The concept of bad victims has been used to reflect on the discretionary judgment made between victims of patriarchal violence, differentiating between those who had honorable behaviors and those who did not. Bad victims are those whose personal and intimate lives interfere with the public's perception of their murders. Their lives serve as a justification for the violence they suffered, demonstrating that, for society, some lives matter more than others. However, this justificatory attitude is not based solely on what the victims did in life or how they managed their sexuality, but also on issues of class and race. The deaths of poor, dark-skinned women seem less outrageous and can always be explained by something other than the macho voracity of their perpetrators.

Pelusa, Vanesa, and Marcela were the worst victims, not only because they were travestis, but also because they were sex workers. After their murders, the press published stories about their sexual morals, behavior in public, mental health, and nighttime habits. All of them have been violated twice, first in the moment of their deaths and then in the way the media treated their lives. Perhaps this is why memory eludes them or prefers to narrate their lives by placing them in the role of passive victims of social conditions that overwhelm them. This is not a new debate for travestis, who have often had to suppress their differences in order to fit in with society's expectations.

In an interview conducted in 2001 with Lohana Berkins, Nadia Echazú, and Marlene Wayar (Alvarez & Fernández 2021), the differences within organizations regarding how to publicly present their demands are discussed:

> Lohana: But Nadia, Nadia Echazú, I'm going to remind you of something, to see if you remember. When we split up, it wasn't just about money. What started to divide us was when we began to appear on television and the ATA women wanted us to say that we were secretaries, hairdressers, and whatever else. It was a heated debate.
>
> Nadia: If you ask me now, my position is clear: there should

be a right to choose, travestis should have the opportunity to have a job. I'm not going to use the term 'decent work,' although I believe that prostitution is also decent work, but prostitution is also a right. I accepted that I worked in prostitution, but I did not defend prostitution at all. And we had accepted things that we would not accept today, such as wearing pants so that the police would not take us away. In other words, we gave in to a lot of things that, in reality, never served any purpose. Even with pants on, they took us to jail anyway. We thought that if we wore pants, since they are not a very feminine garment, we could stop the police, because ordinance 2F referred to scandal in public for anyone who exhibited themselves in public wearing clothing contrary to their sex.

Lohana: The debate went like this: when we started appearing in the media, we discussed what we had to do and how to say it, what we were going to defend. And one group, which still included Wendy [Leguizamón], our comadre, said that when asked about our profession, we had to say seamstress, hairdresser, whatever, but we couldn't say we were prostitutes. Nadia argued that we did have to say it, and so did I, but the difference was that I argued that we had to say why we were prostitutes.

The debate over the image that should be presented to the public and whether or not to associate with the sex work were central to the construction of the trans movement and are still today a source of discussion and division within the trans community. In these debates, victims may or may not fit in with the projects and agendas of the organizations. Although we believe that memory is a pristine and clear space, it is also filtered by these debates, which cause us to remember some cases differently from others. Many memories have been set aside or subjected to rectifications that allow them to be framed within the parameters of what is memorable (Pollak 2006). For example, many later narratives that remember Pelusa, Vanesa, and Marcela avoid talking about their link with sex work or even their struggle for safe spaces to do so, choosing instead to narrate their deaths as the end product of a prostitution system sustained by the patriarchal order. Telling the stories of Pelusa, Vanesa, and Marcela as mere passive victims allows their reconciliation with the demands of the trans activism of the present. These interventions over the memory occur in many cases, especially when it comes to racialized and lower-class people whose biographies took place outside the formal mechanisms of political activism. Pelusa, Vanesa, and Marcela can't be remembered as heroic trans women; trans memory has left them only the role of victims.

*A Memory Without Fear of Contradictions*

We always want to put all the pieces of the historical puzzle together and construct a closed and ordered history about the development of activism. We long to bring order to experiences and place them in a controversy-free space where they validate the discourses of the present and strengthen the demands of the political agenda of organizations. But travesti lives constantly escape classification, the logic of cataloging; any operation we perform on them will inevitably be a cut, a bias, a raw scar on the skin of our narratives. That is why we must constantly engage in the task of working on trans memory, letting go of all previous concepts and venturing into contradiction.

Travesti's lives are complex; they are the most brutal expression of marginalization. Their outsider status should not be suppressed in the ways we tell history, because it is precisely in there where their critical value lies. On the margins, boundaries are blurred, discourses become entangled and collide with everyday experience. The stories of Pelusa, Vanesa, and Marcela are proof of this. They are the expression of lives marked by urgency, with little time to pause and engage in the debates that take place in political debates. The voracity of hunger has led them to build shelters in the night, in partying, in consumption, and in enjoyment, regardless of anything else. Not only is it impossible to explain and order these lives, but it would be deeply violent to try to channel the unbridled power of their lives into a heroic and progressive narrative.

Ultimately, all travesti lives are intertwined and connected. From the most promiscuous to the most saintly, we are all affected by the violence of a world that considers us monstrous. We can manipulate our history to make it coherent or narrate the complexity and diversity that exists within our community, where debates are not so important when faced with cold, hunger, premature old age, illness, and death. A collective and open memory requires us to make an effort to account for the differences and contradictory twists and turns of our lives. If there is no place for whores and scandalous travestis in the hall of fame of trans activism, we must build our own memory and history on the streets where we work.

# A Transsexual Voice on Sexual Politics: Adventures Following Karina Urbina's Documentary Trail

Between 1991 and 1997, transsexual activist Karina Dora Urbina became a key voice in the formation of nascent LGBT activism. Her coalition with activists from the gay and lesbian, human rights, and feminist movements allowed her to build a political strategy to raise awareness of the transsexual people and the rights that the Argentine government denied them. Demands for gender recognition in IDs, access to 'sex change' surgeries, and the right to employment, education, and healthcare were the main statements of her activism.

Her concern about the apartheid situation in which transsexual people lived was reflected in The Transsexual Voice, a newsletter edited by Karina Urbina that can be considered the first publication entirely dedicated to trans issues in the region. Press clipping and other documents reveal her political stance on the emerging LGBT movement, in which she actively participated during its early years. However, a curious collection of letters and personal notebooks provides information about her criticism of lesbian, gay, and travesti organizations.

In this text, I aim to examine in detail the discursive production of this key activist who, almost ten years before her peers, shaped a political narrative for trans(sexual) citizenship. I will also delve into the tensions that Urbina highlighted with her contemporaries, which allow us to better characterize a very particular sexual politics, whose reverberations would impact the history of subsequent travesti and trans activism.

In addition to these interpretations of transsexual activism, I propose to present the methodology of a research project that combines various types of documents, located in different archives and accessed by following an intricate map of clues, traps, and hints. In an adventurous way, the trail of Karina Urbina's documents is strewn with breadcrumbs that mark a key path to understanding the successes and failures of trans politics in Argentina and the Southern Cone.

I.

My introduction to Karina Urbina came through the few references to her in the few academic texts that chronicled the process of organizing the first Pride Parade in Buenos Aires. Among the organizations and individuals mentioned in that significant event for the nascent LGBT community, the presence of the T always seemed to be missing, and Karina's name appeared there, as a necessary addition to give coherence to the history of a community. References to Urbina in other academic texts did not exceed a couple of sentences, at most a paragraph summarizing her political career: Karina Urbina was a transsexual activist, founder of the association Transsexuals for the Right to Identity and Life (TRANSDEVI), who participated in the organization of the First Pride March in 1992. Her activism focused on demanding the right to have her identity recognized in official documents, access to formal employment, and gender affirmation surgeries.

Nothing else. The texts seemed to have forgotten Karina's other facets. So, seduced by this silence, I set out to investigate those missing traces, that elusive stubble of memory. In this text, I will speak in an intimate tone, because I intend to narrate an adventure rather than a strictly academic investigation. It's my personal adventure through Karina Urbina's personal archive, her concise stories, and other archives that I was able to uncover with the permission and complicity of this particular activist from the 1990s.

Another inspiration for delving into Karina Urbina's archive was reading Jay Prosser's book Second Skins: The Body Narratives of Transsexuality. Some of the questions Prosser asked in that text seemed interesting for understanding the void in LGBT history represented by the few paragraphs dedicated to Karina. Prosser critiques queer theory and how the categories used to name sexual identities have been simplified, but also how they are thought about and interpreted (Prosser 1998). His critique of umbrella categories such as Queer and Trans questions the erasure of binary identities that are subsumed within that structure. The paradigmatic example used by Prosser is precisely transsexuality, which, from a post-structuralist and queer theory perspective, is seen as an outdated, medicalizing, and psychiatrizing category and therefore absorbed into trans. But do all people detach themselves from these characterizations? Is it possible for all trans people, in not-urban contexts or fragile material conditions, to be reflected in ideas such as queer identity? Well, no, people simply construct their identities around the categories available at each time and place and according to their social contexts. Nor is it mandatory (or possible) for all trans people to identify with non-binarity, gender rupture, or sexual disobedience. Sometimes people just want to fit in, go unnoticed, and get on with their lives in a safe environment.

Prosser's reflections and critiques helped me understand and expand on some of my previous research questions. I had always been concerned about how sex-work abolitionist feminism placed limits and guidelines on the historicization of travesti activism in Argentina. Now I began to wonder whether the predominance of queer theory had relegated transsexual activism to oblivion by considering it binary, backward, and pathologizing. So I set out to investigate Karina Urbina and her organization TRANSDEVI, looking for the causes she championed, the political initiatives she demanded, and how the connections that led her to participate in the first LGBT parade had come about. My first research resource was the Marcelo Ernesto Ferreyra documentary archive. As a member of Gays for Civil Rights and organizer of that first demonstration, Ferreyra had kept press clippings and other documents produced by Urbina. The clippings portrayed Karina Urbina's participation in several events before and after that march, which allowed me to gauge the extent of her activism over several years, from 1991 to at least 1994.

Parallel to Karina's activism, I discovered the existence of a profuse transsexual activism during the same period, led by other activists: Yanina Moreno, Patricia Gauna, Alejandra Costa, and Mariela Muñoz. Several of these cases were similar to Karina's: the transsexuals differentiated themselves from travestis and emphasized their inclination toward femininity by performing maternal, sensitive, and fragile roles. They presented themselves to the press as women born in the wrong body, unequivocally reaffirming their desire to undergo genital surgery and crying. This image of sensitivity and fragility often legitimized them as women. Clearly, they were not and would not be sympathetic figures for feminists, since, as some radical feminists would say, they 'reinforced gender stereotypes.' This characterization, and the fact that they openly confronted travestis, is central to understanding why they are not enshrined in the pantheon of trans activism leaders.

But Karina was particularly smart. One of the documents treasured by Marcelo Ferreyra showed a nuance. A small orange-covered notebook with only 24 pages recorded that first Pride Parade in a comical tone. In the style of a fanzine, portrayed with magazine clippings and some handwritten notes by Karina, her view of the march and the internal issues that marked its creation. This document revealed a mischievousness, a special perspective, and a capacity for self-reflection on the central role that their activism played in the history of the movement itself. This collection also included letters that Karina had sent to newspaper editors refuting the versions they gave in their publications, dialogues between Karina and Gays DC, and her dissenting views on the decisions made by other organizations. An interview she had given to Sam Larson, editor of K-Bumm Magazine, previewed the publication of a The Transsexual Voice magazine that would feature ideas, reflections, literary texts, and other works produced by members of the transgender community.

This last piece of information led me to two amazing collections of documents. With the help of Juan Queiroz, who runs Archivos Desviados, we accessed some letters that

Sam Larson had received from Karina Urbina, in which she recounts her impressions of the activism of the time. We also recovered three copies of the magazine published by TRANSDEVI called The Transsexual Voice from Queiroz's personal collection. These other documents no longer collected the voices of the press about Urbina, but rather Urbina's first-hand opinions and ideas. From them, I discovered that Karina had a critical view of the direction that activism was taking at the time. She did not feel represented by 'trans' activism, but she also disagreed with some of the strategies adopted by Carlos Jauregui and Gays DC. In one of the issues of La Voz Transexual, she renounces the electoral alliance that Jauregui has formed with Advanced Democracy Front Party and distances herself from Gays DC. But the text also reveals an innovative and forward-thinking strategy: Karina gathered letters of support from various human rights organizations at the time of the founding of Transdevi. Among them, she had the support of the Delegation of Israeli Associations of Argentina, Mother and Grandmothers of Plaza de Mayo, the Peace and Justice Service Foundation led by the Nobel winner Adolfo Perez Esquivel, and others. All of them expressed their solidarity with the struggle of transsexual people for the right to identity and access to healthcare. This also expresses Karina's clear commitment to understanding the issue of transsexual rights within the context of human rights. In some photographs held in the Sarmiento Editorial Collection of the Mariano Moreno National Library, we can see Karina holding signs that read *"no to apartheid,"* equating this term used in the racial struggle with the social ostracism to which transsexual people were reduced. In her interview with K-Bumm, Karina also points out that many transsexual people had to go into exile during the last military dictatorship or go underground for fear of repression. This is one of the first examples of a problematization of the limits of the young democracy in relation to trans identities.

II.

In April 2021, I published an initial text summarizing the results of my research and narrating Karina Urbina's political biography. Before this publication, I received news that Karina was still alive and using a Facebook account. I decided to write to her and send her my text so that she could know that I was working on it and what approach I had taken to her biography. I did not receive a response for several weeks. A few months later, still distressed by her lack of response, I thought that Karina might not be seeing her chat and that it would be better to write a private post where she could read me. I did so, and shortly thereafter I received a response from her. Our communication became more frequent every day, but always elusive. Karina had distanced herself from activism with considerable discontent, according to one of the letters she sent to Larson in 1997. Moreover, after years of remaining in the shadows and almost invisible, suddenly I was exposing her story. She never told me whether she liked the article or not, but we didn't stop talking either, which is perhaps a clue that she wasn't unhappy. In these casual conversations, I discovered more everyday aspects of Karina: her musical tastes, her favorite places in the city, her artistic friendships, her connection to some feminists, her interest for pets and veganism, the precariousness of her material existence, some details about her neighborhood, childhood anecdotes, and stories about her mother. I also discovered that Karina, although she had chosen to be invisible, remained a keen observer of the current state of LGBT activism. She almost never answers my questions, only talking to me capriciously about the topics she prefers on each occasion, but I got used to reading between the lines and identifying clues in her stories. Eventually, I sent Karina photographs and clippings that I found. That's how I once mentioned the little notebook 1992 to her. She told me that when they held the first parade, some magazines had published comics about the event, and she decided that she could make a comic herself and tell her version of that story. That same afternoon, I rushed to the newspaper library and requested all the graphic humor magazines that were available, and sure enough, Satiricón magazine had published a graphic chronicle of that event. So I came to understand that in that casual, pressure-free conversation with Karina, she would drop clues for me, like someone scattering breadcrumbs along a path in the middle of a forest.

When I set out to write another piece about Karina some time later, I discovered that a central part of what I had written in 2021 was wrong. Although the loose ends I had tied up led me to believe that Karina had filed a lawsuit to change her documents and undergo 'sex change' surgery, when I read the court records of that case, I realized that the plaintiff was not Karina, but another anonymous transsexual who was reluctant to speak to the press. This case had a negative court ruling in 1989, but it was reported in the press in 1992. At that time, Urbina was already a visible leader of transsexual activism, so the press confused her with the real plaintiff. In fact, Karina took it upon herself to deny these reports to a newspaper editor, but the misrepresentation persisted and actually served Urbina well in publicizing her activism. Karina and I once talked about it, and she simply told me that at the time, many people were afraid to speak out, so she lent her voice to their cause. Further investigation into the case finally led me to the name of the plaintiff in that case and to a magnificent story of struggle that took place in the corridors of the courts and remained invisible in our history. I still wonder if I will be able to unearth that story without desecrating it.

During one of my visits to Rosario, among the papers documenting the First Travesti, Transsexual, Transgender, Lesbian, and Gay Conference held in that city in 1996, I found a letter written by Karina. I wasn't looking for anything specific, but I suspected from some things I read between the lines in our chats and from some of the things she said to Sam Larson in her letters that I might find her words about this event. Surprisingly, that letter was there waiting for me, with Karina's complaints and discomfort about not being included in the event and about the preeminence given to the voices of travestis. Karina ended her letter with a forceful statement: *"only time will reveal who the true activists were."* I felt that a Karina from the past was now speaking to me through the letter, telling me between the lines, *"it is your duty to bring these words out of silence and make them history."* Recently, Karina sent me a chat message telling me that she had a huge archive of personal photos, banners, sexology books, documents, and newsletters: *"I would have given it to you... It would have been useful to you. It wasn't until 2016 that someone asked me why I knew I had that. But many years have passed."* Time devoured that archive in 2006, during a severe storm that flooded Karina's precarious home.

This adventurous journey through Karina Urbina's personal archive constantly raises questions about how we might construct a trans perspective on archives and the methodology we use to approach them. We are not just objective observers of these documents, but are intertwined with them as part of the community. It is like unearthing the roots of our own existence, bringing other senses, other experiences, and other emotions into play. My little trail of breadcrumbs through Karina's archive is both self-discovery and political learning. I think about the uniqueness of this experience and the possibilities of putting it in dialogue with the pretentiously sterile, yet necessary, practices of academia. This combination of closeness and distance enables us to focus on important categories and practices. Like two lenses of a camera that regulate the rays of light, one academic eye looks from one angle and the other trans eye adjusts from another. It is neither an overflow of emotions nor a chronicle pasteurized in cis language.

On the other hand, the delay between my interest in Karina's archive and its existence makes it necessary to consider what strategies we, the very few trans academics, can use to address the increasingly prolific field of archives and collections that bear witness to the history of our community. Travestis and trans people produce innovative ways of bearing witness to the precariousness of their existence every day, However, academia is too slow to intervene in these documentary collections. Does our absence turn these materials into memorabilia rather than historical documents? Isn't it time for memory to become history?

Karina Urbina protesting outside the Supreme Court, 1991

SOMOS
PERSONAS
CAMBIO DE SEXO
EN LA ARGENTINA
Y RECONOCIMIENTO
LEGAL
SEÑORES JUECES
NOS MARGINAN
AL DENEGAR
NUESTRO DERECHO
A LA IDENTIDAD

Karina Urbina and Yanina Moreno, 1995

Karina Urbina protesting in the National Congress, 1993

Karina Urbina and
Patricia Gauna, 1993

A travesti flees from the
police while taking off her
clothes in protest, 1996

Cover page of an collection about "males vedettes", 1983

Travesti's Front in a demonstration, 1986

Mariela Muñoz detained by the police, 1993

Mariela Muñoz and her partner in a patrol car, 1993

A group of young travestis in detention, 1989

# Newspapers Articles and Op-Eds

# Open Letter to the Females of the Human Species

Dear female human beings of the Argentine Republic. Having been informed of the recent presentation made to the National Institute of Statistics and Censuses (INDEC, for the Spanish acronym Instituto Nacional de Estadisticas y Censos) and the Public Prosecutor's Office, requesting a series of modifications aimed at preserving the *"purity of the male and female categories"*, arguing that "*sex is not assigned by the hegemonic culture nor is it clinically attributed or diagnosed, nor is it a matter of generosity or discernment, but rather a material reality,*" I hereby respond openly and in detail to all the fallacies, insults, and violent, fascist, and transphobic expressions contained in your presentation.

The signatories of the document are renowned feminists and intellectuals from the upper middle class: María José Binetti, PhD in Philosophy and Associate Researcher at the Interdisciplinary Institute for Gender Studies at the Faculty of Philosophy and Letters of the University of Buenos Aires, historian Graciela Tejero Coni (Director of the Women's Museum, member of the Honorary Advisory Council of the Ministry of Women, Gender and Diversity), lawyer Julieta Luisa Bandirali (president of the Women's Commission of the Buenos Aires Lawyers Association), philosophy professor and psychology graduate Valentina Cruz, and lawyer and mediator Marisa Andrea Piumatti (director of the Institute for Legislative Studies of the La Plata Bar Association, member of the group "Women in Law"). Representing women "*of the human species, human beings,*" and adult females," they appear before Federal Court No. 12 for contentious administrative matters to file a claim that basically consists of three points, and I quote:

1- REMOVE the categories "woman," "trans woman," "man," and "trans man" from the gender identity options on the census form, both for the paper form and the digital form. No self-perception should affect or confuse the legal registration of female and male sex.

2- RESERVE the category "gender identity" on the census form for people who identify as "trans," that is, those whose bodily experience does not match the sex recorded at birth. Specifically, the answer to this question should not be mandatory.

3- - REWORD the question inquiring about "gender identity" in accordance with the above request, in the Census Form that will be used in both the digital and in-person versions and for both private and collective dwellings (located on page 3, question 3) as follows:

According to gender identity, the following is considered...

Trans/travesti femininity: a person who, at birth, was registered as male and currently self-identifies as a trans woman or travesti (regardless of whether or not they have changed their ID card or undergone any physical procedures).

Trans masculinity: a person who, at birth, was registered as female and currently self-identifies as a trans man (regardless of whether or not they have changed their ID card or undergone any physical procedures).

*Non-binary: refers to a person who does not identify within the male/female gender binary and instead identifies as non-binary.*

Although at first glance, the plaintiffs seek to camouflage their transphobia by proposing an alternative survey on trans identities, throughout their presentation they make it clear that their main interest is to preserve the category of women only for "*biological women*". They emphasize that *"neither woman nor man are gender identities. They are sexes,"* meaning that they are bodies that have "*the biological, anatomical, and physiological characteristics that differentiate women from men."* They also emphasize that "*there are no trans women or trans men. There are women and men."* Their entire paper does nothing but highlight the superiority of their identities, justifying themselves on biological grounds and attacking gender in a rude way on the understanding that it is a social construct subject to arbitrariness.

The text drafted by Binetti and her supporters constantly insists on the need for the census to accurately reflect reality and to express the actual number of women in society, which in principle would not be a problem with the current wording of the census. Despite the criticism among trans activists, the census continues to record sex in a binary way in the question "*sex assigned at birth.*" This question exists precisely  in order to continue expressing historical comparisons, since one of the functions of the census is to show change and continuity in the characteristics of a country's population. Censuses are dynamic, constantly changing tools that must account not only for numbers, but also for the successes and failures of public policies over a ten-year period.

In this sense, it is impossible to deny that since the last census in 2010, feminist demands, gay and lesbian movements, and travesti, trans, and non-binary activism have reconfigured the ways in which the state addresses the issue of sex and gender. It has been 12 years of transformation. This cannot be eradicated simply by resisting those who seek to uphold the biological imperative, while ignoring the incessant theoretical discussions that denounce the social, political and economic frameworks underpinning the cisheterosexual matrix.

The human females who subscribe to the demand, however, pretend to be unaware of all these advances. They literally declare that:

> The category of 'gender identity' introduced by the Yogyakarta Principles has reinterpreted gender as a deep feeling that defines people and that therefore must be recognized and protected rather than eradicated. Sex, on the other hand, would be something extrinsically assigned by the hegemonic culture. But it must be made clear that the so-called Yogyakarta Principles are nothing more than the expression of the wishes of an NGO. These "principles" do NOT constitute an international covenant to which the Argentine State, or any other state, has agreed. Therefore, they have no legal entity or binding force whatsoever.

A posteriori, they question Article 2 of Gender Identity Law 26.743, which defines gender as "a self-perceived experience that is not subject to medical or legal scrutiny." Not satisfied with this, using some confusing definitions from CEDAW, they attempt to point out that "Gender Identity Law would become unconstitutional and those norms that refer to it as a *basis would follow the same path, as would be the case with the administrative acts that created the census questionnaire."*

Can a group of members of the human species, who are upper-middle class, academics, and white-skinned, claim the power to challenge the current legislative frameworks that have been voted on by the Argentine Congress? Is there some special power emanating from their biological bodies that empowers them to seek to place their ideologies above those decisions legitimately taken by the democratic order of a sovereign nation?

The lawsuit expresses concern that the inclusion of the question on gender identity would alter the data obtained by the census: *"As things stand, instead of providing reliable socio-political information, the Census will contribute to the confusion and distortion of the legal category of 'sex', defined internationally by verifiable and scientific standards, and to the ambiguity of the information collected for statistical purposes."* However, it ignores two central aspects. On the one hand, there are various international documents produced by the United Nations Department of Economic and Social Affairs and the Inter-American Commission on Human Rights that insist on the need for states to collect information not only on gender identity, but also on the living conditions of the LGBTIQ community. Furthermore, the census could never be a true reflection of reality, but rather a simple mathematical operationalization of a series of social variables that are constantly changing. And within those variables, denying the existence of trans women and men would be an attack on the current reality and on the legal norms agreed upon by democracy.

Even worse, with these expressions, the plaintiffs reaffirm

their fascist and transphobic thoughts by pointing out that *"What is nothing more than a belief (queer theory), a postmodern narrative that has followers and international funding, but lacks any basis for being considered the foundation for any regulation involving the general population, has thus been elevated to scientific theory. Subjective feelings or perceptions (self-perceptions) of a minority sector of society that do not correspond to the material reality of their bodies have been elevated to mandatory conditions to be met by the general population, as if this were a social and communal experience."* The totalitarian perspective of the trans-exclusionary feminists who subscribe to the lawsuit is far from the spirit of plurality and tolerance that science pursues. They accuse queer theory of imposing itself on society, while at the same time being scandalized by the fact that trans people demand something basic as being respected. They ask us to conform. These human females believe that their numerical superiority empowers them to impose their views on trans people's perceptions, feelings and emotions. This has nothing to do with science; it is simply a fascist, anti-democratic position that promotes hatred of trans people.

How long? How far? How much longer do they intend to trample on democratic order and the political advances of feminism and travesti and trans activism in the region? Why do they feel that their biological condition entitles them to challenge the scientific output of other people? I believe we need to show that all these pretensions and pedantries of a group of white, university-educated, upper middle class women scientists ARE NOT SCIENTIFIC, have no logical argumentation, and do not defend any material reality. They are simply defenders of the status quo and sexual hierarchies based on biology. They refuse to share the category of *"gender identity"* with us trans people because they consider themselves superior to us. They believe that their vulvas are the incontrovertible argument for not being asked about their gender. If the census instrument fails in any way, it is in having placed male and female without the prefix cis, assuming that we trans people are the rare, the deformed, the inadequate ones.

I am not entirely comfortable writing this open letter. I know that I am exposing myself to direct attacks from those mentioned in the article and also from the growing number of TERF. But I am convinced that our silence does not help to minimize the fascist advance of these sectors. We have already belittled those who spread their hatred on social media, we have marginalized them and treated them as mere confused Twitter users. But they are not. Facts such as these show that these are people and groups who are very well positioned within feminism, who hold positions in universities and organizations, who sit at the table of the Ministry of Women, and who are undoubtedly financed by the same international capital that supports the emerging Latin American neo-fascisms and the parties that, disguised as liberalism, promote a conservative ideology. Today it is a lawsuit, which has taken place in a federal court. Very soon these will be initiatives that form coalitions with the many conservative and fascist politicians who occupy TV screens, spewing hatred against trans people and spreading falsehoods. We must remember Lohana's thoughts when she insisted that we must defend the inalienable right of our travesti bodies. We must raise our fists high and respond with travesti fury that THEY SHALL NOT PASS! NEVER AGAIN!

# Crossroads and Challenges for "Recognizing Ourselves" in the Trans Population Statistics of the 2022 Census

*"The life expectancy of trans people is 35 years"*… Who has not heard this statistic repeated every time the reality of the travesti and trans people is discussed? This statistic has become one of the central statements of trans activism in Argentina and become a key piece to achieve public policies in favor of our legal recognition and integration into the workforce. This data highlights our vulnerability and effectively informs civil society about the situation faced by trans people. However, statistically recording the trans population has always been a dilemma, even for the activists that have undertaken the task in coordination with state agencies and academic institutions.

*Background, Pilot Tests, and Trials for Compiling Statistics*

The first statistics in Argentina for the trans and travesti population were precarious surveys carried out by the victims themselves. During the 1980s, many travestis were murdered on the Pan-American Highway in the most brutal ways. Although the news flooded the tabloid newspapers, little is known about the total number of deaths during the period 1983-1993. Debora Singer, a popular travesti and actress at the time, reported in the newspapers that a dozen women had been killed in 1987. Other travestis reported figures that climbed to a hundred. Beyond that, there are few details and it is difficult to reconstruct that figure by scrutinizing court records, as many of the victims have been registered under male names and filed as accidental deaths. In fact, often the bodies were not even claimed at the morgue by family members and the funerals were left to other travestis friends.

It was not until 2005, following the publication of The Feat of One's Own Name , compiled by Lohana Berkins and Josefina Fernández, that the first systematic data on the living conditions of travestis, transsexuals, and trans people became available. This publication brought together data obtained through surveys conducted in the City of Buenos Aires, some towns in the inner suburbs of Buenos Aires, and the city of Mar del Plata. The data was recorded using questionnaires that were implemented in a non-random manner (i.e., the sample was delimited based on the research criteria, aiming to interview a specific group: travestis, transsexuals, or trans people) in group interview settings. The organizations that participated in this first survey were the Association for the Struggle for Travesti and Transsexual Identity, Transgender Future, Anti-Discrimination and Liberation Movement, among others. Later, in 2008, the publication of Cumbia, Guzzling, and Tears made it possible to expand on the data obtained previously as a total of 300 questionnaires were included, which also recorded data from the provinces of Córdoba, Salta, Mendoza, San Miguel de Tucumán, and Neuquén. In this way, the data commonly known about the life expectancy of the trans population in our country was constructed, along with much of the statistical information that was available at the time of the debate on the gender identity law.

In 2012, INDEC conducted a pilot study of the trans

population in the district of La Matanza in collaboration with social organizations, involving more than 200 respondents and a dozen trans interviewers trained by the agency . More recently, in 2017, The Butterfly Revolution was published, paying tribute to the first publication by Berkins and Fernández and updating the statistical data, incorporating two central issues: the effects of the enactment of the Gender Identity Law and some statistical data on trans masculinities (Defensoria del Pueblo CABA 2017). However, this report focuses primarily on the City of Buenos Aires. Some provinces have compiled their own statistics on trans people, including Salta, San Luis, Misiones, Santa Fe, and Buenos Aires. In 2019, the "Survey Manual and Questionnaire" was presented, prepared by the National Office of Comprehensive Sexual Diversity Policies under the Ministry of Human Rights for the purpose of conducting a national survey of the trans population, which had its first pilot test in the city of Paraná (Instituto Nacional de Estadística y Censos - I.N.D.E.C. 2019). The report on this pilot test, in which 60 people participated, provides results that allow for a more accurate understanding of the current living conditions of the trans population.

*Methodological and Sampling Difficulties*

Almost all of the studies mentioned above highlight the enormous difficulties involved in surveying the trans population. One of the most obvious challenges is sampling, i.e., defining the universe of cases to be used during the research. These difficulties stem from our general lack of knowledge about the number of trans people in Argentina and their location. Therefore, it is extremely difficult to define the sample and specifically target the trans population: we do not know how many people there are, where they live, or where they usually go. For this reason, most research has been conducted in cooperation with trans organizations, as their "native" knowledge allows them to define a specific sample. The technique used to conduct the trans population surveys is known as snowball sampling or chain-referral sampling: a reference person is interviewed and asked for information about other people who could answer the same survey, thus exponentially increasing the number of respondents with common characteristics. This methodology is usually the most effective for several reasons: on the one hand, it allows access to populations that, due to their small size, could not be found probabilistically in the general population; and, on the other hand, due to its specificity, it is the most accessible and fastest way to produce statistical data. The great difficulty with this technique is that there is a lot of room for sampling bias to be introduced as a result of the perspectives of those conducting the research or providing data on potential respondents, which leads to a greater difficulty: the impossibility of generalizing the data obtained.

In the case of the statistics compiled to date, the collaboration of trans organizations has been central. Not only have they participated by providing guidance on defining the sample, but they have also contributed fully to the development of the statistical tool. In many cases, as Lucía Fuster Pravatto recounts, *"...we sought to incorporate the voices of the trans people who joined the project throughout the process, not as voices to be used in terms of testimonial narrative, but as critical and political interventions. The reading of the original survey and the decisions made to incorporate changes to it, as well as the interpretation of the* data, the fieldwork, and the preparation of the final report, were all collective decisions, the product of deliberation and consensus." The result of this joint effort between activism and academia has led to an increasingly accurate understanding of the trans population vulnerability.

Another difficulty that must be taken into account when conducting research with the trans population is the need to create a friendly and respectful interview environment that allows data to be collected in a context of trust. Otherwise, the data may be inaccurate, making it difficult to obtain reliable information. For this reason, in most of the surveys conducted, interviewers were trained in advance on best practices for working with the trans population, the Gender Identity Law (particularly the section on dignified treatment), and the laws that protect statistical confidentiality and seek to prevent the identification of survey respondents. In this regard, the "Survey and Questionnaire Manual" emphasizes that: *"During the interview, a relaxed atmosphere of trust and intimacy should be created to make it easier for the interviewee to provide personal information. To this end, you should express yourself clearly and fluently, appear confident, and treat the interviewee in a friendly and respectful manner."* Attached to these recommendations are the instructions and procedures for obtaining informed consent from respondents.

In this same way, one of the common criteria in the surveys already conducted has been to hire trans people as interviewers, thereby ensuring that the encounter with the respondents is friendly and conducive to the interviews. In the case of the surveys conducted by Berkins and Fernández, the roles were filled by colleagues from the organizations that took part in the research, and in the case of The Butterfly Revolution, the surveyors were students from Mocha Celis and volunteers from the Gender and Sexual Diversity Program of the Public Ministry of Defense of CABA. In the pilot test carried out in Paraná, five trans women and one trans man conducted the interviews.

*The National Population, Households, and Housing Census*

The National Population Census is the fundamental tool of the National Institute of Statistics and Censuses. In the presentation to the 2022 Census Operating Committee, they emphasize that the census is *"a well-established mechanism that, every decade for more than a century, has produced the basic information that allows the State at its three levels, national, provincial, and municipal, to plan public policies, monitor them, and evaluate their results. The information it provides is also a tool for analysis and decision-making in the private sphere."* The census is also the measurement of the Argentine population that allows for the estimation of annual budgets and, therefore, the amounts that should be allocated to each governmental office (Grandis 2021) . For this reason, the census is central to all the gender policies that feminist movements have firmly demanded in recent years.

The current National Population Census has been disrupted by the Covid-19 pandemic, as it could not be carried out in accordance with the 10-year frequency established in Article 47 of the National Constitution. This is not the first time that this irregularity has occurred, as in both 1991 and 2001 the censuses were carried out a year later due to the economic crises that marked the beginning and end of Menem's neoliberal policies. The census currently planned will be the

11th in Argentine history. The first was conducted in 1869 under the presidency of Sarmiento and the last in 2010, coinciding with the surprise death of Nestor Kirchner. Over time, the Census has measured a multitude of variables and used various methods.

The first censuses were conducted in a very rudimentary manner and excluded indigenous peoples who were not considered inhabitants of the Argentine Nation. For many decades, the census did not record the children of single mothers or common-law marriages, among other curiosities. Gradually, the census became institutionalized and began to investigate the characteristics of the population with greater precision. Each modification to the census reflects the State's interest in capturing a more accurate snapshot of the actual population. The current population census incorporates several new features: it will be the first national census based on legal rights, meaning that it will register each person in the place where they have rights and obligations arising from their residence (payment of taxes, access to health care, right to public space, etc.) It will also be the first census to be conducted using a mixed method that combines the traditional census system of collecting data directly at the place of residence with the use of a digital platform that will operate for several months prior to the traditional census. This tool will be called e-CENSO and will allow people to complete the census form in advance.

The latest innovative addition to the current census, and one that draws attention in this article, is the question on self-perceived gender identity, which will be included in order to comply with the changes introduced following the enactment of the Gender Identity Law. The inclusion of this variable is not new on the international scene, as it has been introduced in other censuses, although not without resistance from trans activists who oppose the ways in which this is applied.

*Gender Identity in National Censuses: The Case of the United Kingdom*

In 2018, the Inter-American Commission on Human Rights made a number of recommendations to Member States, including the importance of *"implementing policies for the collection and analysis of statistical data on violence and discrimination affecting LGBTI people, and on the various aspects of the lives of lesbian, gay, bisexual, trans, and intersex persons (e.g., education, work, housing, health), in coordination with all branches of government, in a disaggregated and systematic manner; and to use such data in the design, implementation, and evaluation of government actions and policies aimed at these individuals, as well as to formulate any relevant changes to existing policies,"* especially in population censuses (Comisión Interamericana de Derechos Humanos 2018). The UN made recommendations along these lines in 2019, which prompted INDEC to incorporate measurements in this regard in the 2022 Census. At the same time, documents from the United Nations Department of Economic and Social Affairs have emphasized the need to record sex: *"The census questionnaire should record the sex (male or female) of each person. The breakdown of data by sex is a fundamental requirement for gender statistics. Many of the socioeconomic and demographic characteristics that could be collected through a census, such as education, economic activity, marital status, migration,* disability, and housing arrangements, often vary by sex. In this context, the presentation of sex-disaggregated data is important because of its use in gender studies." (Principles and Recommendations for Population and Housing Censuses 2017)

Population censuses are sensitive to changes in society, which means they are constantly under pressure from new population structures and the legal contexts of each country. In fact, the 2010 census recorded same-sex parent households, reflecting the change introduced by the equal marriage law. Some countries have already introduced questions about self-perceived gender identity, for example Australia, New Zealand, and Canada, while others, such as Argentina and the United Kingdom, are in the process of incorporating such questions. In the United States, there are also initiatives in this regard that are currently under public debate.

The case of the United Kingdom is perhaps the most useful for considering the tensions that the census will generate in our country. Guided by international recommendations, the Office for National Statistics decided to include a question on gender identity in the national census, which was conducted virtually in March 2021. The question asked was: "Is the gender you identify with the same as the sex you were registered with at birth?" If the answer was no, respondents could state their self-perceived gender. The question was optional and only available to those over the age of 16. Even so, the inclusion of this question sparked controversy, mainly because it implied that each person had to disclose their trans status. The controversy over what data to make visible and what benefits and dangers detailed information on the trans community might entail gave way to an offensive by sex-based feminist activists, who intervened in the dispute to such an extent that they filed a complaint with the Supreme Court against the ONS, demanding that it include instructions such as that the question on 'sex' should be based on official documents, such as birth certificates. For trans-exclusionary feminists, the option provided by the question on gender self-perception 'guided' respondents to answer something other than their biological sex. Most LGBT activist groups celebrated the decision to be counted in the census, despite the difficulty of doing so, as they considered that the inclusion of questions that make the trans and LGBT population visible explicitly acknowledges their existence among the citizenry and allows for the development of more effective policies. Under the hashtag #ProudToBeCounted, the LGBT community celebrated being included in the census.

In the United States, there is some resistance to the inclusion of questions about sexual orientation and gender identity, due to past incidents that violated the confidentiality of census data. The rise of conservative sectors has put the American LGBT community on alert, given the possibility that the data could be used to persecute the community or single out LGBT individuals in a potential scenario of conservative governments.

Far from unambiguous positions, the international scene has shown how activists have adapted their reception of census measures to the contexts in which they occur. While remaining alert to the possibility that statistical mechanisms may violate the confidentiality and privacy of certain data, in some contexts priority has been given to the possibility of constructing reliable data that challenges perceptions and can show the advances and setbacks of policies on the rights of trans and queer people.

*The 2022 National Census: Horizons, Challenges, and Possible Approaches*

The development of the statistical survey for the 2022 Census has required a great deal of work. Work began well in advance, analyzing a set of variables that must be taken into account for the Census to be carried out effectively, including international agreements and recommendations on the subject, current statistical paradigms, the legal frameworks in force, and, above all, the eventual reception of respondents and the technical limitations in its application. The preparation of the Census requires balancing all these elements in order to construct reliable statistical information that can be compared historically.

This is a key point that restricts some of the decisions that can be made in relation to statistics. The variable 'sex' is considered one of the basic variables, as it provides useful information for gender policies, but it also underpins the processing of census information. The bell curves featured in the graphic, which are based on data from each census, are organized according to a binary representation of gender, and modifying them would alter the historical comparative analysis of the population. This is not a minor issue; in fact, it is highlighted as a central issue in the working documents and proposals made by INDEC for the current census.

The 2022 Census is built around the slogan "*Recognizing ourselves*" and aims to construct a new paradigm in census matters that tends to humanize statistical data. The central question is not the traditional one about the number of people living in the country, but rather about who we are, what characterizes us, and what constitutes us as a population. 'Recognizing ourselves' will be key in this complex statistical survey process, and it is within this paradigm that information on gender identity, ethnic affiliation, and Afro-descendant heritage takes center stage. In addition, the 2022 Census seeks to generate integrated information at the national level, that is, information that can be compared and systematized with other existing statistical records, which is another reason why some historical variables must be preserved.

However, there are some necessary considerations regarding how gender identity will be measured. The census will include two questions on this issue: one at the beginning of the form, which will ask about the sex registered at birth and can only be answered with 1- male or 2- female, and another towards the end of the census, which will ask "According to your gender identity, do you consider yourself…" to which you can respond with one of the following six options:

1- Trans woman/travesti

 2- Trans man

3- Woman

4- Man

5- None of the above or

6- Ignored.

These two questions attempt to balance the methodological difficulties of the census, on the one hand the need to maintain the historical variable 'sex' that allows for historical comparison, and on the other hand to introduce other forms of gender identity that allow for an account of the current state of the population and the design of specific policies for trans people.

The way the question is presented has at least two problems: the question about sex puts the respondent in a position of 'confessing' sensitive and personal information; and the options provided in response to the question about gender identity are imprecise and incomplete, which could lead to confusion and measurement errors. Furthermore, unlike the UK census, the question about gender identity is not optional here.

Asking about the sex assigned at birth violates the Gender Identity Law, as established in Article 9: "*The rectification of sex and change of first name in the registry shall not be made public in any case, except with the authorization of the data subject.*" Furthermore, it violates all good practice guidelines and recommendations aimed at eliminating the stigmatization and pathologization of trans people. If the survey is conducted in this manner, census participants should be asked to provide special authorization or sign an informed consent form detailing the principles of confidentiality and non-individualization of statistical information in accordance with Law 17.622. On the other hand, respondents could answer this question by referring to the sex recorded on their amended birth certificates, as this is the only document that records such information. In that case, it would be difficult to distinguish the trans population within the overall population, and problems would also arise in the case of non-binary people who have obtained amended certificates that include other identity attributions or where the sex field is left blank. It is worth remembering that the form must be filled out according to the respondent's answer and cannot be completed automatically by the interviewer, although in practice, due to haste or discomfort, this field is often filled out incorrectly according to the interviewer's criteria. It is therefore essential that the 600,000 volunteers who will participate in the Census are properly trained on the correct treatment of trans people and the guidelines for collecting this data.

The field that records gender identity presents terminological and methodological difficulties. On the one hand, it makes the mistake of reducing the broad spectrum of trans identities to just three broad categories: trans woman/travesti, trans man, or other. While this third option allows the question to meet the conditions of exhaustiveness that all statistical variables require, it renders invisible the non-binary and transsexual communities that warrant specific measurements. We already know that the possibility of leaving fields open has been questioned on other occasions, for example in the especial decree that makes documents with an X viable, but in the statistical instrument, an addendum could be considered in the "*other*" field that allows for the declaration of a generic affiliation, which would make it possible to know with which terms the trans population identifies. In fact, the UK population census allows specific affiliations to be recorded in some fields. In this sense, the incorporation of virtual tools such as e-CENSO facilitates the task of data collection and systematization. Last but not least, it would be noteworthy for the male and female options in the question on gender identity to specify that they refer to CIS males and females, in order to stop categorizing trans people as abnormal. It is understood that an addendum of this type poses a challenge in view of the lack of training on gender issues, but this could be remedied with the proper training of volunteers.

In summary, in order to adapt the statistical instrument to the demands of the trans community, it would be important to make some modifications that would make the interview situation more pleasant and encourage participation. The census, with the fields as they are currently presented, hinders trans participation or requires a type of exposure that is not always comfortable. Can we trust that the interviewer's engagement is sufficient guarantee that the data will be provided in a climate of trust? Not in a machine as massive as the national census, which mobilizes more than half a million interviewers. Even in the best scenario, it will be difficult for such a large number of volunteers to be sensitized to such a degree that the rights of trans people are not violated. At the same time, statistics are necessary for the functioning of the state and, in particular, for the design of public policies that affect the trans community. It would be a mistake for the current design of the instrument to discourage participation, especially in a scenario where exclusionary trans feminisms, in alliance with conservative sectors, threaten setbacks in trans policies.

Just as the Census is fraught with tensions, our activism must also be strategically planned and in dialogue with the context of the region, which forces us to set aside some of our radicalized positions in order to build public information. It will be difficult to get through the 2022 Census without facing contradictions. On the one hand, it is understandable that organizations, ministries, and other state agencies require statistical data to support public policies. On the other hand, there is the desire of trans people to preserve their identity anonymously. We have activism focused on demanding affirmative policies from the government, but at the same time we have large sectors of the population that distrust the state, which, far from being generous, has been the perpetrator of historical patriarchal violence. This problem also confronts us with the limits and crossroads that identity-centered activism has created: we have organized our demands around the particularities of our identities, and now we are at the center of the panopticon. Women and LGBT people have demanded specific policies for our communities that recognize us and make us visible. But visibility, registration, and statistics are the tools with which the state draws the new territories of power. If in classical modernity it was maps and physical territories that were the terrain where the power of the nation-state was disputed, today it is statistics and information that are the space for the realization of biopower, which no longer rests solely in the hands of states, but also in those of large corporations and hegemonic discourses that shape the world order. Our activism must be reflective and mutable, porous and plastic, in order to interact with current contexts, generate demands for the rest of society, and propose collective solutions that transcend individual experience to take root at the intersections where gender policies confront their contradictions.

# No More Jail Time: Preliminary Approval for the Trans Employment Quota Law

If Lohana and Diana had been there, they would have melted into an embrace and become one flesh imbued with emotion, turning into an amalgam of cumbia, guzzling, and tears, surrounded by glitter and sparkles. But we miss them. We miss them so desperately that we even feel a little emptiness in our hearts as we cry, moved by what we have achieved: we have partial approval of the Travesti Trans Employment Quota Law. And although Lohana and Diana were not there, thanks to a kind of travesti alchemy, last night there was fairy travesti dust in the air and we all felt a little of the mystique and emotion of them, our travesti queens.

This chronicle is a personal perspective: it can hardly contain everyone's joy or the opinions of a complex space such as the trans movement. Today more than ever, this story is localized in a very personal place; it is the narration of an experience traversed by my privileges and my reflections. It is the possible chronicle, made up of my own voice and trajectories, which surely intertwine with those of my generation, those who came before me, and those who are coming, ready to bring punk vibes and rebellion to the travesti fury.

My first feeling was nostalgia. When I arrived, the street I expected to be overflowing with colors and flags was empty. Only on the corner of the Congress was a group of comrades taking a photo with flags and banners. I had imagined a scene full of trans people, with Berkins in charge and her booming voice on a loudspeaker. On that sidewalk, I suddenly thought I saw Karina Urbina chained to the railings next to Carlos Jareguí. Working so much with archives makes me think all the time about that generation of activists who put on a majestic performance in the 1990s. Now we have the pandemic looming, and mobilizing becomes a contradiction in terms. In the end, the streets remain hostile, elusive, and unfriendly to us.

When the debate began, Congress was filling up with our bodies. Our brown faces, our disobedient voices, and our footsteps filled the hallways and balconies. We were not an angry mob, nor were we a fiery crowd, but we were present. Due to health protocols, it was difficult to access the premises, and entry was limited to representatives of organizations and their allies. But around 10 p.m., when the debate began in the Chamber of Deputies, we arrived and took over Congress. Our flags could be seen on the balconies. The exhausting afternoon of work was filled with friends, and between coffees, we ventured into different scenarios. From the beginning, there was confidence. This law did not come out of nowhere; it is the product of many years of struggle and builds on the precedent of Decree 721/2020, passed in September last year. This debate was preceded by many hours of work in committees and long days of collective work and discussion, which continued even during the pandemic. There was confidence, but we always have to be on our guard.

A total of twenty-five speakers took to the floor before the microphones and cameras of the Chamber of Deputies. The committee's ruling was read out and the bill was debated in detail. With varying degrees of agreement, all the deputies who took the floor agreed on one key point: the Trans Employment Quota Law is not granting travestis, transsexuals, and transgender people a privilege, but rather restoring a right that has historically been denied them. It is a matter of paying a debt to a sector of the population that democracy has turned its back on with disdain, that is not even allowed to sit down for a job interview, that has not even been given enough hope to write a resume. One deputy asked: How many here have hired a trans person? The answer is so obvious that it becomes a sufficient argument. No one. Reduced to spectacle, sex work, or hairdressing, it is difficult for representatives to imagine that a trans anthropologist is behind this article, putting one word after another to describe her work and our achievement. Representatives from different parties presented their arguments with varying degrees of confidence. Some have clearly been working on this issue for years and have shared their struggles with us. They have trans people on their workteams and really know what this law means for everyone.

Of course, there were those who wanted to teach us about discrimination, attacking us from the left. For opposition lawmakers, the Trans Employment Quota Law, by creating a registry of people who adhere to this identity category, would generate a type of discrimination. But the truth is that if this discrimination did exist, it would be positive, meaning that it would allow for the structural violation of a sector of society, something understood within the current legal framework, to be remedied with affirmative action. But beyond the opposition, which totaled 11 votes against 207 in favor, the Travesti and Trans Employment Quota Law reached preliminary approval yesterday. The speeches also paid tribute to many key colleagues: Lohana and Diana at the top, for the significance of their struggle, but also Claudia Pia Baudracco, Mariela Muñoz, Cris Miró, and so many other colleagues from different provinces who have put their hearts and souls into this debate.

The phone never stopped ringing. My friends from the Abortion Right's Campaign inquired about the progress of the discussion, concerned and knowledgeable about the legislative arena. My travesti friends from Cafayate sent me their Calchaquí strength and asked me to speak up for the vallistas, even though I am a city girl adopted by the sun and wine of those landscapes. At one point during the night, I was overcome with emotion and sent a video message to my colleagues in Salta, thanking them because they were also the ones who put me here. I, who had come down from the hills and settled in my little corner of Buenos Aires, was able to be in the chamber watching a historic moment. I thought of the women from Salta who fought ardently from their unjust anonymity, of Rosario Sansone and Pelusa Liendro. At one point, I received a message from my friend Victoria, her voice breaking. We both trembled with excitement, knowing that in just a few minutes our dream would become a little more real.

At around 1 a.m., the debate ended and voting began. The countdown was a deafening heartbeat that kept us on the edge of our seats. *"This feels like New Year's Eve,"* said one person. *"New Year's Eve for trans women,"* I thought. That countdown welcomed us to a new chapter in history. Perhaps this law will not be enough, it may not be implemented for those of us who are on the verge of our expectations, but it leaves the door open for future generations. We know that after the law is passed, we will still have to wait and fight for the quota to become effective and fulfill its spirit of restitution. But every second less on the clock in the Chamber of Deputies was another moment of hope in our hearts, one second less until we see a future with travestis and trans people retiring, going to the doctor, taking the subway to work. And who knows, maybe one second less of waiting until we see a travesti representative in Congress speaking in the first person about our history.

The countdown ended and the alchemy worked its magic. The veils fell and we saw the votes: by a large majority, we achieved the preliminary approval of the law and with it, half of a long-awaited victory. We cried and hugged each other, cries burst from our throats and applause erupted. I looked down and saw the representatives standing in the chamber applauding us. Congress was completely transformed for a few seconds; the rectitude and solemnity of those corridors was tinged with our flags, and the boxes, barely occupied by the few of us who were able to enter, were filled with the multitude of absences that are part of our lives. There, alongside us, were the thousands of comrades persecuted by edicts, those exiled, those beaten by the police, those killed during the dictatorship, those thrown out onto the streets, those abused by their families. There were thousands of us on those balconies. We were suddenly liberated by fury and sang with more conviction than ever: no more jail time!

# Where There Is a Right, a Need Arises: Challenges Regarding the Enactment of the Trans Employment Quota

Last night, the Senate voted on the Trans Employment Quota Law, which establishes that 1% of national government jobs must be assigned to trans people. This law is the result of more than a dozen bills that were presented by various political parties and activist groups. After a year of committee work, and following Decree 721 issued in September 2020 by the executive branch, the bill reached the House of Representatives on June 11, where it received 207 votes in favor, giving it the green light to move on to the Senate. Last night, after several hours of debate, the Travesti and Trans Employment Quota finally became law.

The Employment Quota Law establishes the following actions and commitments on the part of the State:

*1- The target population of the law is defined as travestis, transsexuals, transgender people, or persons who do not identify with the gender assigned to them at birth.*

*2- It is established that the agencies of the three branches of the national government, autonomous entities, and state-owned companies must employ a proportion of no less than 1% of their total staff as trans employees without this implying the termination of existing employment relationships.*

*3- Educational attainment should not be an obstacle to the hiring of trans persons, as long as they commit to* completing their studies or accessing relevant training during the course of their employment. The means must be provided for applicants to access the training required for the job.

4- Misdemeanor records shall not be taken into consideration, nor shall criminal records that do not represent an obstacle to job performance.

5- The quota must be complied with in all obligated agencies, taking into account a federal geographical distribution of job positions.

6- Awareness-raising actions must be taken to ensure the effective integration of trans people in state agencies.

7- Priority in hiring shall be given to private companies that comply with the trans employment quota. Likewise, an incentive system shall be available for private companies that hire trans people, with employer contributions being credited against national taxes for a period of 12 to 24 months.

8- The National Bank shall have a system of accessible loans for business and co-op led by trans persons.

9- The creation of a single registry of applicants for the trans employment quota, as well as the confidentiality of the data entered in this registry.

10- The promotion of the participation of trans people representing trade unions and civil society organizations in monitoring the implementation of the law.

11- The creation of a Coordination Unit composed of

*representatives from the Ministry of Women, Gender, and Diversity, the Ministry of Labor, Employment, and Social Security, the National Institute against Discrimination, Xenophobia, and Racism, and the Ministry of Education.*

*12- Inviting the provinces, the Autonomous City of Buenos Aires, and national universities to comply with the provisions of the trans employment quota law.*

*13- The law must be progressively implemented within a period of no more than two years from its enactment.*

These points are the result of a consensus among a plurality of projects presented, but also of the trans movement's deep reflection on the limitations of quota projects in provinces and institutions. It should be remembered that there are other provinces where quota laws have been passed for years without having any significant effect, as well as universities and state institutions where trans quota projects have rarely gone beyond a mere rhetorical formula declaring good intentions. The trans movement has learned the hard way that one swallow does not make a summer and that often, even when the dog is dead, the rabies does not end. Similarly, we are forced to rethink the Peronist maxim pronounced by Eva Perón: "*Where there is a need, a right is born*" and ask ourselves what needs are born where a right has been won.

The law's passing is a victory. It is the foundation on which new achievements and political horizons for our movement must be built. Just as the Gender Identity Law was a big achievement for trans people, the Trans Employment Quota Law inaugurated a new way of thinking about the links between trans people and the government, through formal employment, even under the precarious forms of hiring that currently exist. This relationship raises many issues that must be mentioned and observed because they challenge the horizons we hope to overcome in the near future.

One issue that necessarily arises after reading the law is to re-discuss who are the subjects of cissexist oppression. The wording of this law refers to travestis, transsexuals, and transgender people and avoids explicitly mentioning non-binary identities, transmasculinities, and other categories that are emerging as necessary in the ways of naming current and (perhaps) future trans experiences. In this sense, the trans employment quota law gives legal status and produces a cut in the ways of naming one's own experience that the Gender Identity Law had taken care not to make explicit. Lohana Berkins reflected on this issue when raising the discussions within the Gender Identity Front and said the following:

There was no need to define different identities because we didn't have to impose on future generations whether they were travestis or trans or whatever. It could happen that they wanted to embody another identity and we didn't have to tell them. Each person had the right to choose who to be and what to call themselves. Transvestism, transsexuality, and transgenderism are understood in a multitude of ways and in a variety of modes and expressions. Giving a closed definition could have meant that many people would have been left out of this benefit of the law. That was when we decided not to use any categories, and the way we found to get out of that discussion was with the concept of gender identity.

What will it mean in the future for current law to move toward a closed definition of trans identities that differ from the objectives of the Gender Identity Law? It is quite obvious that in the relationship with the state, whose fervent historical vocation has been the registration of populations, a restricted way of naming identities has had to be established. The power of the notion of gender identity embodies an ungovernable abundance, which in the quota law is limited for the purposes of ordering, classifying, and registering individuals who will be eligible to receive the right to affirmative action policies for formal labor inclusion. In the short term, this may not be a problem, but in the long term, we face the challenge of giving this issue its proper dimension in practice so that the state's vocation for registration and governance does not end up undermining what the notion of gender identity meant for our freedoms and desires. This is especially true because the restrictive wording of the law threatens to create divisions, differentiations, and hierarchies within the trans community itself.

Although quota laws are presented as affirmative action policies that offer a minimum percentage of hiring for historically disadvantaged sectors, in practice these floors often end up being ceilings, something that must necessarily be reviewed in terms of actual application, taking into account other quota experiences that unfortunately have not achieved their stated objectives. Quotas for people with disabilities, for example, established by Law 22,431 passed in 1981, 40 years ago, are not only not effectively enforced throughout the country, but often do so without real integration. It is important that the law establishes the importance of awareness-raising as part of the actions to be taken, because often accessing a job through a quota system produces a feeling of rejection, paternalism, disability, and even disdain among the rest of the workforce. The purpose of this project is to promote the integration of trans people into formal employment, and this will only be possible if this 'inclusion' is achieved on a basis of real equality, without discrimination.

One point included in the projects that generate discussion was the importance of involving trans people in monitoring the law. Although it is established that trade unions and civil society organizations may participate in this monitoring, it would be important for this working group to be open to other voices, such as trans people from universities and independent activists who have no ties to partisan or state-linked organizations and who can act as observers of the ways in which hiring takes place, the criteria used to establish priorities among applicants, and other aspects that may cloud the selection criteria. It is important to remember that the government is not a sphere separate from civil society and that it is constantly under tension and permeated by disputes and forces that intersect with the interests of the market, political parties, religious institutions, etc. This trans participation must be made explicit in the regulations of the law, because although this government has a Ministry of Women, Gender, and Diversity that employs trans people, it is likely that future scenarios will dispense with such diverse compositions, leaving the application of the law to governmental office that is unaware of the community's demands. Trust in the state and public policies is becoming increasingly common within feminism, but we must remember that our historical trenches have been in the streets and not in the elegant offices of government power.

Although this law represents progress in terms of access to employment, it is still important to discuss at least some of the issues that were raised in the speeches made within the legislative chambers. It has often been said that this law comes to repair and pay a debt to travestis. Reference has been made to the history of codes of misdemeanors that criminalized our identities. It has been said that this is a law that grants rights to a group forgotten by democracy. But the truth is that, as it is currently formulated, this law is significant for a part of the trans population with active employment potential and not for all of our community. For those travestis who have worked on the streets in conditions of secrecy and moral condemnation, who have suffered police persecution, who have experienced firsthand the neglect of the medical system that systematically threw them into hormone therapies and homemade surgeries, for those travestis this law is more of a symbolic victory than a real achievement. Is it possible to think of demanding that colleagues who suffer from severe health conditions and bear the physical scars of violence integrate into formal employment? Is it not necessary to move forward with real projects of financial compensation for those forgotten by democracy? There are projects in this regard that have sought to reach the congress without success and that must be seriously discussed if deputies and senators intend to honor what has been said in parliamentary work.

One final issue that is not addressed at all in this law deserves to be discussed as soon as possible. We can't talk anymore about trans labor inclusion without a legal framework regulating sex work. Trans labor promotion and inclusion policies seek to offer options to the travesti, transsexual, and transgender community that has historically been associated with the sex work, but at the same time, it is necessary to fix the legal status of those who choose it as another equally valid labor alternative for the material resolution of their lives. It is entirely understandable that this law, named after two important abolitionist trans women, avoids these discussions, especially considering that its objective is to promote formal employment, but this does not make it less urgent to discuss new legal rights for sex workers. If you have ever spoken with trans sex workers, you have probably heard phrases like this: "*If I can work on my own and earn enough in one night or one weekend to support my lifestyle, why am I going to work eight hours a day cleaning the floors of a government office? Is a formal job going to give me enough to support myself?*" This economic rationality is unquestionable, but it also encapsulates a political stance on the limits that employment within capitalism offers. We must not forget that formal employment is always a bond of subsumption. Being workers within capitalism does not make us free, but rather subjects us to the logic of efficiency, profitability, and institutionalized morality. It is impossible to deny that for many travestis this law represents the hope of getting off the streets and projecting themselves into another model of citizenship, but it remains unknown that there are ways of managing material things, desire, and the symbolic resolution of life that escape the established forms of 'work' within this modern, colonial, and capitalist society.

This note has no other purpose than to raise questions, pose problems, and venture challenges. It does not seek to undermine the resounding victory that this law represents, but rather to bring to the table the questions that many of us have kept quiet out of discretion and strategy. Now that the quota is law, we are called upon to devise new battles, rethink strategies, rebuild trenches, and reclaim the streets, everyday life, encounters, and dialogues. We have made great strides in recent decades, embracing feminism, lesbians, gays, bisexuals, queer, and intersex people. We have held the same flag high through all the tensions of the winds and hurricanes. Now that everything seems calmer, it is time to return to the critical value of our differences and reinforce our ships for the storms to come.

# X Is the Answer: Argentina Moves Forward in Recognizing Non-Binary Identities

In mid-2020, following the premiere of the TV show *La Veneno* about the life of Spanish trans woman Cristina Ortíz, a debate broke out on Twitter between Spaniards and Argentinians regarding the categories used to refer to the show's protagonist. The contenders accused each other of reproducing a pathologizing perspective of trans identity by using the category 'transsexual,' which emerged from psychiatric studies on sexuality in the mid-20th century, or of using a derogatory and insulting term by referring to her as a 'travesti.' Some proposed naming La Veneno as a trans woman, adopting a category that emerged from activism in recent decades.

The fruitless debate highlights the murky terrain of sex-gender identification when national borders are transcended. The identity of travesti, which for Argentines and some countries in the southern cone of Latin America is a category full of political power thanks to activism such as that of Nadia Echazú, Marlene Wayar, and Lohana Berkins, is an insulting and aggressive term for other countries. The word 'transsexual,' which for some embodies the legacy of pathologization, has been a valid category, for example for Karina Urbina and Argentine transsexuals in the 1990s. Geographical and historical distances distort the possibility of capturing identity experiences in a single word, or perhaps our identities are and will always be a gender that is impossible to describe and record exhaustively.

With the enactment of Decree 476, the Argentine

government seeks to fix a complex set of difficulties that arose after many people demanded to be registered in a way other than the male/female binary currently in use. The first case occurred in Mendoza, following a lawsuit filed by Gerónimo Carolina Gonzáles Devesa, they obtained a correction to their birth certificate from the provincial civil registry, which removed any gender category. However, as I pointed out in a previous article, in Argentina each province makes their own birth certificates, then the national government issued ID cards that reflect the information contained in those certificates. The lack of rules about the national ID cards system regarding modified birth certificates carried several problems for trans people. Between 2018 and the present, rectified birth certificates were issued in the provinces that did not specify gender or specified various designations: self-perceived, non-binary, undefined, etc. This meant that a large number of cases accumulated of people who, despite having obtained the rectification of their birth certificates, were unable to obtain an ID card that recorded these designations, due to the technical and bureaucratic challenge this represented for the national government .

In mid-2020, during the pandemic, joint working agreements were signed between the Ministry of Women, Gender, and Diversity and the Ministry of the Interior to advance the processing of these documents. It was Victoria Tesoriero, head of the Secretary of Political Affairs of the Ministry of the Interior, who brought the activists' demand to Minister Wado De Pedro, who in turn forwarded the proposal to the president.

Today, these efforts are finally taking shape in this decree, which essentially establishes a new item in the sex category of ID cards where, in addition to M for male and F for female, the letter X will be included to encompass identities that are *"non-binary, indeterminate, unspecified, undefined, unreported, self-perceived, unrecorded; or any other meaning with which a person who does not feel included in the male/female binary could identify."*

**Why an X?**

Many years ago, I removed the gendered declension from my own name and adopted it as a political statement. Today, I consider myself a travesti and would not mind having a X on my ID card. However, after much reading and research, I realized that having an ID with that X could only respond to part of who I am and provide answers only for certain contexts of my life. Part of living our travesti freedoms is being able to imagine ourselves in utopian places and futures, and I have also dreamed of myself, and in those dreams, IDs are only instruments.

We must ask ourselves what IDs are and what they are for, in order to understand their limits and specificities. IDs issued by the state fulfill specific functions that are far from producing a complete synthesis of our identities. Fundamentally, IDs are tools: they serve the state to collect information considered useful for the social life of the population. The president said it during the presentation of the decree: *"What the State is interested in is registering Alberto Fernández, knowing if he fulfills his tax obligations, knowing if he doesn't launder money, if he doesn't commit crimes, that's what matters... Why does sex matter?"* IDs and official documents produced in and by the State serve the purpose of recording and keeping a record of certain aspects of its citizens that are useful for life in society. No more, no less.

The issue of identifying individuals goes far beyond nation states and is governed by international guidelines and provisions. The decree clearly and thoroughly outlines the international agreements and conventions to which Argentina is a signatory and which it must therefore comply with when issuing ID cards. It is important to note that many "first world" countries have made progress in this regard, for example Canada, New Zealand, and Australia. Many countries where there are culturally different ways of naming genders (India and some Middle Eastern countries) also have a third category to record something other than the male/female binary. On June 30, 2021, the U.S. Department of State announced that President Joseph Biden had ordered the prompt implementation of a third category in passports and official documents in order to respect the rights of non-conforming identities and the LGBTIQ+ community. All these international provisions have created an important scenario that allows Argentina to move forward with an identification system that recognizes other ways of experiencing gender outside of hegemonic masculinity and femininity.

But at the same time, this international scenario presents opportunities and restrictions: documents (and in particular travel documents) must fit into international standards and must be readable by automatic devices in accordance with current technologies. This is why the X emerges as the best option, due to its widespread use internationally. Undoubtedly, the response proposed by the Argentine government with this X is fraught with limitations, but it is a rational, studied, measured, and safe response to the possibility of continuing to make mistakes that further bog down the situation of those who demand a document that fully represents them. It had already been imprudent, albeit bold, on the part of the provinces to issue certificates that could not then be validated by the national government, leaving hundreds of people outside the law. Would it not have been imprudent to also issue documents that include gender designations that could not be recognized outside Argentina's borders? The decision taken today and carried out by the Ministry of the Interior appears sensible and logical, even though it continues to obscure important issues.

*Does the Government Care About People's Gender?*

In his speech, the president asks: "*Does the state care about people's gender?*" It turns out that yes, the state does care about people's gender. Feminists have long denounced state interference in our lives and the role that the modern, patriarchal capitalist system has played in our private and public experiences. Alberto Fernández's speech, peppered with slogans recently annexed to the political agenda of his administration, speaks innocently of the state, ignoring the fact that its function has been and continues to be to control its citizens. Sex has always been of interest to the state. Sexual difference is the matrix on which many of the structural and structuring inequalities of the system rest. And this is a widely studied and denounced reality, which a state that proclaims itself feminist should not turn a blind eye to. Far from cheering Fernández's words proclaiming the necessary abolition of gender, we must observe the evolution of public policies with caution.

Although as feminists we have denounced for centuries the way in which sexual difference condemned us to second-class spaces and placed us in the realm of caregiving and reproduction, we have also based our activism on this difference and in recent years have achieved a series of rights and victories that necessarily address the peculiarity of our identities. Without gender categories, many of the public policies and rights we have won would be meaningless. The Gender Identity Law itself would make no sense, nor would the struggle to be recognized as subjects of abortion, quota laws, the law on the prevention of gender violence, etc. The entire framework of our demands is based on the use we have made of the categories with which the master subjugated us and which today are the platform for our struggles.

It is in this sense that we must understand that our IDs are a tool and not a government certification of who we are. Official documents and legislation should serve us in achieving those dreams; we must be able to use them to move around, to shop, to collect payments, to vote, to have abortions, etc. In short, they should serve us in inhabiting society and democracy. After that, our identity, if there were a final and true one, is our most private property. We put it into play in our beds, in our bodies, among friends, with our children, in the places and experiences that matter to us. For it to be our property, for us to be able to retain it as intimate and our own, is to step out of the panopticon a little, to escape a few miles from power.

In that controversial and debated X, in that intriguing and complex X, we may have a way out. As in an equation, X is a secret value. It allows us to half-undress and leave doubt, intrigue, questions, and secrets behind. It allows us to continue being inhabitants of that other world, of that place of our own, where the only certainties we have are that we want to build other ways of living. The X allows us to declare what we are not without telling governments who we actually are, and that is fine for now, because sometimes not everything that is named exists, nor does everything that exists want to be named.

# Bodies with the Capacity to Desire

"*I am interested in showing why travestis, transsexuals, and transgender people can contribute to the National Campaign for the Right to Abortion. (...) We also produce knowledge, we can develop theory, and in this sense, I insist, we are not proposing to change the focus of the central, fundamental issue, which is women, but rather to enrich this Campaign and this proposal by working on issues that are part of the same question, such as taking away the ownership of our bodies from states, corporations, and churches.*" (Berkin 2010)

Driven by the fervor of the feminist waves, it is sometimes difficult for us to observe and remember what brought us here, at what point in our lives the spark was ignited that fueled the heat of our struggles and that today is this burning fire that contains us all. The rhythm of our lives, steeped in obligations and slogans, forces us to be subsumed into the relentless machine of progress, where there is very little time left to look back and recognize the origins of the paths we use today, but which were inaugurated by others. Today we are on the verge of celebrating a law that allows us to have abortions, that allows us to decide about our bodies and reaffirm ourselves as the inalienable owners of our sexuality. We are a short distance away from a law that draws a new sexual frontier and declares us sovereign over our desire.

But we did not arrive here accidently, pushed by the waves, stunned by the strident green of the scarves. We got here through a history of struggles that can be read from different perspectives and from which different excerpts can be made, but in all of them, a special chapter must always be dedicated to the National Campaign for the Right to Legal, Safe, and Free Abortion. There have been previous experiences and incursions outside the Campaign that have also been successful and noteworthy, but if anything led us to where we are now, it is that we all made a coordinated effort. We put our partisan convictions aside and built a network full of tensions, differences, disagreements... but a network nonetheless. And we all know that in Argentina, that's extremely hard.

We came together in a single movement and recognized each other, looked each other in the face, and realized that we were diverse. We were a multitude and we were many. Unable to be reduced to a single category, we declared ourselves as the green wave. And we dressed ourselves in green scarves. Over time, we imprinted the memory and strength of our mothers and grandmothers of Plaza de Mayo at the center. We turned an object historically associated with tears into an emblem of freedom and relentless struggle. We embellished our scarves, embroidered them, and passed them from hand to hand as a secret code among comrades. And we stamped them with the flag of pride when we understood that women were not the only ones affected by abortion.

In recent weeks, criticism of the bill and its handling has proliferated, especially due to the cissexist nature of many of the statements made by deputies during the presentation of their arguments. The anger is understandable, because in this struggle, travestis, trans kids, lesbians, queer, and non-binary people have been actively involved from the beginning, and it becomes exhausting to hear the debate go round and round in circles, ignoring our experiences. But despite everything, the last three drafts of the bill include identities beyond the binary. Although it may seem like little, for some time now the use of the category 'pregnant person' has permeated other regulatory frameworks and is included in various bills, which shows that some of the work is bearing fruit.

It is also important to remember that the debate on abortion has always been restricted and tense. This debate often goes beyond our wishes as a political movement and is limited to party and state agendas. The discourse on abortion is in itself a knot of tensions where every word counts. Where we would like to talk about desire, we are told that abortion is a last option. Where we would like to talk about autonomy, we are told that it is a public health issue. And where we would expect to be named, capricious categories slip in: pregnant person, pregnant bodies, identities with the capacity to gestate, etc.

Even so, we have built in parallel, together, in alliance with feminists, a common agenda that allows certain debates that seemed distant a few years ago and now are printed on the political agenda of party spaces, activist groups, and the media. The Green Wave energized many discussions that had been going on for some time and were urgent, especially regarding the cissexist and heterocentric positions of many feminists for whom the travesti and trans experience was alien and distant. Creating this alliance with feminist movements was already in the minds of leaders who were fundamental to our struggles, such as Lohana Berkins, who in 2010 recalled how she had encountered the struggle for abortion and what had mobilized her to take a place within the Campaign:

> "We began to take up an issue that was not directly our own, but we did see the demand for bodily autonomy as an absolute right. (...) That claim to bodily autonomy (in this case, women's right to decide whether to have children, when to have them, why to have them, and with whom to have them) resonated deeply with us: 'We want our bodies so we can transform them, live them, show them off, or whatever else we want to do with them.' I think that's when we first glimpsed the issue of defending sexual rights and, later, reproductive rights."

Lohana and the other travestis understood with great clarity that the debate was not only about the ability to gestate or the desire to abort, this struggle was also about our bodily autonomy and the right to freely dispose of our sexuality. Abortion, seen as more than just a reproductive issue, led queer people to join this fight and make significant contributions by holding heated discussions within the Campaign to change ways of thinking and demand a right understood as "belonging to women." These debates were not easy, but they were undoubtedly fruitful. Today, the Campaign brings together many queer, gay, lesbian, and bisexual comrades around the Sex-Gender-Political Dissidence Collective and other networks who understand this right as the platform on which to build new decision-making autonomy over desire.

The participation of lesbian activists was central to developing a strategy to support those who wanted to have an abortion. Between 2009 and 2012, the Lesbian and Feminist Hotline for the Decriminalization of Abortion accompanied nearly 10,000 abortions and collectively developed protocols for the use of misoprostol, which proved to be extremely important in removing abortion from the hegemony of the medical system. The guide Everything You Want to Know About How to Have an Abortion with Pills [*Todo lo que querés saber sobre cómo hacerse un aborto con pastillas*] is practically an independently published best seller. Thousands of copies were distributed at the National Women's Meetings, and there were an estimated 200,000 downloads from the sites where it was originally uploaded. However, it undoubtedly circulated from hand to hand, photocopied and replicated thousands of times, accompanying those who needed information to manage their own abortions. The experience also brought out of the closet the fact that women have abortions and do so in a way that is different from how it had been represented until then, as pointed out by Mines, Diaz Villa, Rueda, and Marzano, former members of Lesbianas y Feministas:

> *The fiction that "no one wants to have an abortion," which is upheld as politically correct discourse, contradicts everyday reality: there is one abortion per minute in our country. The imposition of silence behind the statement "No one wants to have an abortion" seems more like a threat to women themselves than a political argument. What is hidden behind the statement is the desire to have an abortion. It is hidden because it seems impossible to accept that there is agency in the experience of abortion. There is autonomy and self-determination. There is a desire that is fulfilled. It is true that rarely does anyone become pregnant with the intention of having an abortion but once pregnancy occurs and the decision to abort is made, desire appears. This desire may*

*run counter to feminist logic, which speaks little of desire and more of destiny, as if destiny were to become pregnant without wanting to and to abort without wanting to. Perhaps because we understood this desire, perhaps because as lesbians we shared something of the experience of desire that ran counter to the norm, the hotline was definitely a revolutionary political act for every woman and each one of us." (Mines Cuenya et al. 2013)*

Transmasculine activism made significant contributions to the debates surrounding abortion. On the one hand, it sparked a profound discussion about reproductive justice and the need to question the procedures and interventions to which trans bodies were and are subjected in order to be recognized and legible to state agencies, which often leads to surgeries and treatments that result in compulsory sterilization. On the other hand, this exposes the multiple forms of violence to which transmasculine identities are subjected when they turn to health systems in search of gynecological and obstetric care. Another central point of the issues raised in relation to abortion was the experience of the organization Putos Mal, which, under the slogan "Legal abortion for trans gay men," called for a rethinking of the presumption of heterosexuality among trans men. Many of these debates took shape in the 2016 Campaign project, which, although it did not achieve parliamentary status, presented "people with the capacity to gestate in accordance with the provisions of Gender Identity Law No. 26,743" as subjects of the right to abortion.

In the debates and demonstrations surrounding the abortion debate in 2018, trans-masculine activists intervened with posters and flyers exposing many of these issues and generating their own language in which bodily autonomy, the right to decide on pregnancy, and ways of experiencing sexuality took shape in provocative graphics. The Trans Masculinities Front also intervened, questioning the lack of participation by trans people in committee debates and denouncing the cissexist bias of many of the presentations made. They also presented points of connection between the right to gender identity won in 2012 and the demands for the right to abortion. Fernández Romero highlights the experience in his work:

> The Trans Masculinities Front also drew parallels between abortion and gender transitions, some aspects of which were facilitated by the Gender Identity Law; they framed both issues within a broader spectrum of decisions about one's own life and one's own gendered and sexualized body. They affirmed, "We are the owners of our bodies. To choose our names and pronouns. To decide whether or not we want hormones and surgery. To decide with whom to have sex or not. To choose whether or not to gestate." Just as the Gender Identity Law made it possible for decisions about gender and body to cease to be the prerogative of judges, doctors, and psychiatrists within the framework of a pathological understanding of trans identities, in their flyers they asserted that decisions about gestation should not be in the hands of health professionals or any other external agent. (Fernández Romero 2021)

This article can hardly summarize all the interventions that trans, non-binary, and other queer people have made regarding abortion rights. The very logic of crowds makes many experiences less visible, even though they have tremendous impacts on individual stories. Trans and queer people are part of the green wave and contribute in many ways, accompanying people through abortions, sustaining the struggle in the streets, producing knowledge, questioning the status quo, and participating in debates both inside and outside the Campaign. All of these forms of intervention are valid because they continue to strengthen the network that sustains our desire for a society with new frontiers.

We are not seeking to be at the center of this story, nor are we seeking to make women invisible, as trans-exclusionary radical feminists claim, but rather we are complicating the perspectives used to think on abortion and bringing out of the closet those doubly clandestine trans and queer abortions: penalized by law and considered abject by a heterosexist system.

At the same time, it is necessary to go beyond mere criticism and get involved in some of the many spaces, projects, and networks that work to facilitate and support the wishes of those who have abortions. Only by participating actively is it possible to dismantle the foundations of cissexism, to produce knowledge that challenges it and makes our clandestinity visible. Undoubtedly, the task is not easy, but the reward is enormous and almost within our reach: the possibility of constructing bodies without owners. The conquest of free, libidinal, and autonomous bodies. Bodies with full capacity to desire.

# Kill Joy, Kill Pride: Keys to Disarming the Glitter Bomb

I feel sick. You make me sick. All the middle-class idiots outraged by the ban on non-binary language in Buenos Aires, confident that calling someone 'they' will have a huge impact on the educational trajectories of the travestis who work the streets in a dirty red-light district, shivering with cold and fear. The heterosexual, performative guys who feign outrage at Nicki Minaj's transphobic statements while staring at her tits and sending me nudes on my Instagram account in the early hours of the morning as if I had nothing better to do than make them horny! They make me sick with rage, I vomit with anger, their idiotic tweets get stuck in my throat, and I bite my hands to keep from writing. I escape from so much conformity and boredom by watching cake or fake videos on YouTube, and I imagine you believing the *trompe* l'oeil, because I've seen you believe in the most idiotic illusions. This is my letter of resignation from listening to you, my rejection of the invitation to celebrate another Stonewall 'birthday' with you. The disclaimer I'm going to put on my Tinder profile: I'm not interested in being cool.

Yes, bro. I read your Instagram Stories about how much pinkwashing makes you angry every time June rolls around. I'm sure next week you'll post a photo of Marsha P. Johnson and tell us all how important travestis were in the Stonewall riots, but I doubt you've stopped to think that in Argentina there are some trans women who are just as legendary, if not more so, who are fighting for historical redress for the violence inflicted on them by the state during the dictatorship and democracy. Dudes, my apologies for not being fancier like the drag queens who catch your attention in your clubs full of twinks cut from the same mold. It seems that you never realize that it's not only pinkwashing when Nike paints itself with rainbows, but also when the streaming platform feeds you an gay friendly shows with which you —from your middle-class privileges— flash that Netflix is revolutionizing queer representation on screen. Iconic, you'll say in your proper private school English. But it's nothing more than the sound of a story of struggle becoming merchandise, becoming a partisan statement, becoming a prefix that the normies dumb white feminists will add to the name of their group to say how cool they feel being 'trans-feminists.' And it doesn't matter much whether or not there are trans people in their spaces. The issue is only on the discourse, and the important thing is to transform it to change the world. *"You have to thank Kirchnerism that at least now you can name yourself and have your ID card."* Well... No, my dear!

I don't want to thank anyone anymore, or put on a polite travesti act. I don't want to celebrate, or be happy, or see the bright side of anything. I don't want to hear them say anymore that this shit is the gateway to other rights. They don't realize that all that shit sounds like trickle-down theory, but horizontal, which is just the vulgar promise of a future that never comes. NO, I don't want it anymore. I'm tired of being happy and tired of the crude hope of middle-class progressivism. I'm tired of them talking loudly about access to jobs for travestis while they pay me two pesos fifty for my articles, to be collected in sixty days. I don't want to pretend anymore, I don't want to say that this situation deserves pride and struggle. I don't want to keep dancing to the beat of the glitter bomb whose sparkle only touches the usual privileged who, through inherited privilege, suckle from the deformed and inflated tits of a state that is defeated. I don't want any more.

*"If my discourse is disappointing, even depressing at times, it is not because I enjoy discouraging people, quite the contrary. It is because knowledge of reality leads to realism. One must constantly juggle two roles: on the one hand, that of killjoy, and on the other, that of an accomplice to utopia,"* said Bourdieu (1985). But how can we be accomplices to something that is so far from being a utopia? How can we celebrate these light and vague debates that always take place hundreds of miles above the discourse of material practices? We need a new utopia made of bitter emotions, full rage, and genuine travesti fury. The typical momentary indignation that lasts on social media until a new 30-second clip of Milei or Trump goes viral is no longer useful to anyone. We need anger and sadness to get out of the addictive scrolling that makes us believe that our Twitter debates matter to someone. We need a punch in the face to wake us up, and I'd much rather have you girls give it to me than wake up one day with a right-wing dude smelling of rancid cum pointing a taser gun at my chest.

What is the difference between the illustrations in Jehovah's Witnesses' brochures and the scene in Lightyear where two lesbians kiss? Aren't both images a bourgeois representation of the promise of happiness? I've seen them celebrate and fight on TikTok all week about that tacky, domesticated scene of prefabricated tolerance. "Does gayness bother you, or does the representation of homosexuality as something natural bother you?" says a gay influencer with the mediocre impunity of someone who makes a living selling slogans. NATURAL!? Haven't we already closed that door? That kiss is a caricature. It is a crude representation of what this society expects of us and of the generations that will inherit us: people domesticated by love, family values, and happiness as the horizon of life, people devoted to reproducing the discourses of postmodernity and seized by the capitalist drive for accumulation and success. Alienated people who are not even capable of understanding that their life project is coerced by a civilizing zeal that bears no resemblance to the emancipatory ideas and sexual freedom we once achieved.

We still have time to get up from the table of happiness. Sara Ahmed (2010) says that "*feminists kill joy in a certain sense: they disrupt the very fantasy that happiness can be found in certain places. It's not just that feminists aren't happy with what's supposed to cause happiness, but that their unhappiness is read as sabotaging the happiness of others.*" We can still be an uncomfortable and unfriendly presence that ruins the party for everyone. That should be our new utopia, and our meeting place with feminisms. If there is an intersection where we should be able to meet, it is at the corner of Disobedience St. and Fury Av., to meet to be ballbusters, grumpy, and angry. To tear down all the 'love is love' banners; to shake the glitter off the average sissy who thinks he's so cool for going shirtless at Pride showing off his OnlyFans body; to sabotage the joy of those who think that more Peronism equals more rights. to slap awake heterosexuals who would die of anger if their 'partner' left them to date a trans woman; to the unwary travestis who trust the state because they were given a position as 'secretary of diversity' in a shitty city government. Let's get together to reveal that behind the Monopoly of oppressions that some people like to play so much lies a project of segregation and sectarianism that is absolutely unnecessary and unproductive. We have to get up in unison from the table of happiness and kick the board, bang our fists violently, and leave without further explanation. A blood clot and screams must form in our throats, like Sylvia Rivera in 1973 when she confronted her former gay and lesbian comrades to tell them that it was always them, the street transvestites, who supported the most vulnerable with their efforts.

The thing is, travestis are the ultimate party poopers, the real killjoys. We have thick skin from so much liquid silicones self-injected and shamelessness and so much abuse. So many disdainful looks have turned us into rude, foul-mouthed women. We have satiated our hunger with semen so many nights, we have torn the bitterness from our chests so many times, like tearing thick hair from a beard, that we no longer feel pain or bleed. That's why we are so ungrateful, as Marcia Ochoa (2008) says: "*Trans women have all the reason in the world to be resentful and ungrateful to society. The miracle for me is that not all of them are.*" We are proud inhabitants and citizens of Shame City. We couldn't care less about society's expectations of our bodies and good manners. On the outskirts of civic morality, we gather in Shame City to erect an Empire of scandalous acts. Sometimes we venture into your civilized gatherings of college girls who drink tea and smoke weed. Sometimes we make ourselves pretty and flirtatious so that your pussies and asses don't tremble with fear. Sometimes we write little things to suit your whims, tame erotic stories, very feminist reflections on the intersectionality of our oppressions, but when we are alone we laugh out loud at how stupidly comfortable your lives are and how alienated you live in your studio apartments in the your gentrified neighborhood. You can't imagine how sedative it is to hear you cry about your bourgeois little problems with the cadence of a queer tango.

Our way of inhabiting shame allows us to challenge others and incriminate them. As Kulick and Klein (2009) say, travestis use scandal as a way of reterritorializing shame, of inverting it. Our irreverent and beastly way of living our lives, far from humiliating us, exposes their dark prejudices, their cheap moralizing, their expectations of proper citizenship that slip right off us. This text is an invitation to travestizing feminisms, to prostitute LGBTQ+ spaces, and to produce a new trench that breaks with the logic of pride. I am not even proposing to invite you to a 'critical pride.' It is about us taking it upon ourselves to shame conservatives, to make libertarians tremble, to confront the domesticated members of our own collective, and to make heterosexuals afraid to go out on the street. It is no longer enough for our response to be pride; we have to make them feel ashamed of their happiness and bourgeois comfort.

We deserve a Shame Parade, a parade of obscenities and scandal that highlights all the joy they stole from us, everything we don't have to thank them for. We owe ourselves a national gathering of travestis and killjoys who wipe their asses with history and slogans and applause. We owe ourselves funerals for our dead, tears, snot, anger, and blows. We cannot fall asleep and let the glitter bomb feed on defeated bodies, let them exploit our history to sell stickers, T-shirts, and flags with which capitalist society and its bourgeois morality wipe their asses while promising us that we will be happy. No, I don't want to be invited to the funeral of our disobedient lives. I want fury, gasoline, and fire.

# Bibliography


Ahmed, Sara. 2010. *The Promise of Happiness*. Duke University Press.

Alarcón, Cristian. 2019. "Un crimen de odio en la ciudad del poder." *Revista Anfibia*, June 17. https://www.revistaanfibia.com/crimen-odio-la-ciudad-del-poder/.

Álvarez, Ana, and Josefina Fernández. 2021. "Nadia y sus amigas." *Moléculas Malucas*, February 5. https://www.moleculasmalucas.com/post/nadia-y-sus-amigas.

Álvarez, Ana Gabriela. 2022. "Maricas Chicharras y Travestis: Mercados, Espectáculos e Intercambios Transnacionales En Los Orígenes de La Identidad de Mujeres Trans (Buenos Aires, Años 1960-1970)." *Revista Uruguaya de Ciencia Política* 31 (1). https://doi.org/10.26851/RUCP.31.1.5.

Aruquipa Pérez, David. 2016. La China Morena. la revolución estética de las travestis en las fiestas populares de Bolivia: el inicio de una conquista. https://digitum.um.es/digitum/handle/10201/52644.

Aversa, María Marta, and Matías Máximo. 2021. *Si te viera tu madre*. Editorial de la Universidad Nacional de La Plata (EDULP). http://sedici.unlp.edu.ar/handle/10915/128271.

Berkins, Lohana. 2008. "Un itinerario político del travestismo." In *Sexualidades migrantes: género y transgénero*, Segunda edición. Feminismo y sociedad 1. Librería de Mujeres Editoras.

Berkins, Lohana. 2010. "Intervención Panel 3. El Aborto: Aspectos Éticos, Jurídicos y Político." Paper presented at Seminario Internacional "El derecho al aborto, una deuda de la democracia."

Berkins, Lohana, and Josefina Fernández, eds. 2005. *La Gesta Del Nombre Propio: Informe Sobre La Situación de La Comunidad Travesti En La Argentina*. Madres de Plaza de Mayo.

Blanco, Osvaldo S. 2009. "Biopolítica, espacio y estadística." *Ciencia Política* 4 (7). https://revistas.unal.edu.co/index.php/cienciapol/article/view/16251.

Bourdieu, Pierre. 1985. *Qué Significa Hablar. Economía De Los Intercambios Lingüisticos*. http://archive.org/details/bourdieu-pierre.-que-significa-hablar.-economia-de-los-intercambios-linguisticos-ocr-1985.

Butierrez, Marce Joan, and Mir Yarfitz. 2024. "Trans and Travesti Identities in Twentieth-Century South America." *Oxford Research Encyclopedia of Latin American History*.

Butierrez, Marce, and Patricio Simonetto. 2021. "No Uterus, No Opinion? Travestis, Gays & Maricas' Activism for the Abortion Legalization in Argentina." *History Workshop*, February 10. https://www.historyworkshop.org.uk/queer-history/no-uterus-no-opinion/.

Chomsky, Noam, and Michel Foucault. 2006. *The Chomsky-Foucault Debate: On Human Nature*. The New Press.

Cutuli, María Soledad, and Santiago Joaquín Insausti. 2015. "Cabarets, Corsos y Teatros de Revista: Espacios de Transgresión y Celebración En La Memoria Marica." In *Memorias, Identidades y Experiencias Trans:(In) Visibilidades Entre Argentina y España*. Biblos. https://dialnet.unirioja.es/servlet/articulo?codigo=9773052.

Cytryn, Lucia. 2021. "Aventuras del tercer sexo: Les Girls en Buenos Aires." *Moléculas Malucas*, October 12. https://www.moleculasmalucas.com/post/aventuras-del-tercer-sexo.

Fernández Romero, Francisco. 2019. "Nos sentamos para poder caminar": Luchas travestis y trans por el espacio público en Buenos Aires (1980s y 1990s). In *Libro de Actas del IV Seminario Latinoamericano de Geografía, Género y Sexualidades*. Universidad Nacional del Centro de la Provincia de Buenos Aires. https://ri.conicet.gov.ar/handle/11336/138202.

Fernández Romero, Francisco. 2021. "'We Can Conceive Another History': Trans Activism around Abortion Rights in Argentina." *International Journal of Transgender Health* 22 (1–2): 126–40. https://doi.org/10.1080/26895269.2020.1838391.

Ferreyra, Marcelo Ernesto. 2020. "Ángela Vanni. La matriarca de las travestis." *Moléculas Malucas*, July 10. https://www.moleculasmalucas.com/post/ángela-vanni-la-guardiana-de-las-travestis.

Galeano, Diego, and Cristiana Schettini. 2022. "Contra locas y putas." *Moléculas Malucas*, September 24. https://www.moleculasmalucas.com/post/contra-locas-y-putas.

Henderson, Magally Alegre. 2012. "Androginopolis: Dissident Masculinities and the Creation of Republican Peru (Lima, 1790-1850)." Stony Brook University.

Hiller, Renata, Aluminé Moreno, Ana Mallimaci, and Lohana Berkins. 2007. *Cumbia, copeteo y lágrimas: informe nacional sobre la situación de las travestis transexuales y transgéneros*. Asociación de Lucha por la Identidad Travesti-Transexual, A.L.I.T.T.

Insausti, Santiago Joaquín. 2015. "Los Cuatrocientos Homosexuales Desaparecidos: Memorias de La Represión Estatal a Las Sexualidades Disidentes En Argentina." Débora DAntonio (Comp.) *Deseo y Represión. Sexualidad, Género y Estado En La Historia Argentina Reciente*. Buenos

Aires: Imago Mundi, 63–82.

Kulick, Don. 1998. *Travesti: Sex, Gender, and Culture among Brazilian Transgendered Prostitutes*. Worlds of Desire: The Chicago Series on Sexuality, Gender, and Culture. University of Chicago Press. https://press.uchicago.edu/ucp/books/book/chicago/T/bo3621380.html.

Kulick, Don, and Charles H. Klein. 2009. "Scandalous Acts: The Politics of Shame among Brazilian Travesti Prostitutes." In *Gay Shame*. University of Chicago Press.

Manzano, Adriana Valeria. 2019. Tiempos de destape: sexo, cultura y política en la Argentina de los ochenta. August 19. https://ri.conicet.gov.ar/handle/11336/155284.

Milanesio, Natalia. 2019. *Destape: Sex, Democracy, and Freedom in Postdictatorial Argentina*. University of Pittsburgh Press. https://doi.org/10.2307/j.ctvpwhf9c.

Mines Cuenya, Ana, Gabi Díaz Villa, Roxana Rueda, and Verónica Marzano. 2013. El aborto lesbiano que se hace con la mano: Continuidades y rupturas en la militancia por el derecho al aborto en Argentina (2009-2012). November. https://ri.conicet.gov.ar/handle/11336/28699.

Oberlin, Ana. 2022. "Mujeres Trans y Travestis: Una Gran Deuda Para Tener Una Mejor Democracia." In *Ser Mujer En La ESMA*, II. CELS - Centro de Estudios Legales y Sociales.

Ochoa, Marcia. 2008. "Perverse Citizenship: Divas, Marginality, and Participation in 'Loca-Lization.'" *WSQ: Women's Studies Quarterly* 36 (3): 146–69.

Pollak, Michael. 2006. *Memoria, olvido, silencio: la producción social de identidades frente a situaciones límite*. Ediciones Al Margen.

Prosser, Jay. 1998. *Second Skins: The Body Narratives of*

Transsexuality. *Gender and Culture*. Columbia University Press.

Queiroz, Juan. 2023. "Maricas Unidas Argentinas (MUA)." *El lugar sin límites. Revista de Estudios y Políticas de Género* 5 (9): 229–40.

Rapisardi, Flavio, and Alejandro Modarelli. 2001. *Fiestas, baños y exilios: los gays porteños en la última dictadura*. 1. ed. Ed. Sudamericana.

Rivera, Sylvia, and Marsha P. Johnson. 2013. *Street Transvestite Action Revolutionaries. Survival, Revolt and Queer Antagonist Struggle*. UNTORELLI Press.

Simonetto, Patricio. 2019. *El dinero no es todo: compra y venta de sexo en la Argentina del siglo XX*. Colección Ciudadanía e inclusión. Editorial Biblos.

Solari Paz, Ana Cecilia. 2023. "'aMorales' En Dictadura. Vertiente Material de Las Violencias Hacia Las Disidencias Sexo-Genéricas a Través Del Estudio de Caso de La Policía de La Provincia de Buenos Aires (1976-1983) (Primera Parte)." *Corpo Grafías Estudios Críticos de y Desde Los Cuerpos* 9 (9): 119–38. https://doi.org/10.14483/25909398.20253.

Thompson, Edward P. 1980. *The Poverty of Theory and Other Essays*. 3. impression. Merlin Press.

## Primary Sources

Aguilera, Ivana. 2020. "Peleamos por acceder a los derechos básicos." Actualidad. *CTA Córdoba*, April 25. https://ctaacordoba.org/peleamos-por-acceder-a-los-derechosbasicos/.

Archivo Nacional de la Memoria. 2023a. "Entrevista a: Andreína Di Brino." August 18. Archivo Nacional de la Memoria.

Archivo Nacional de la Memoria. 2023b. "Entrevista a: Julieta González." August 9. Archivo Nacional de la Memoria.

Archivo Nacional de la Memoria. 2023c. "Entrevista a: Perica Burrometo." September 13. Archivo Nacional de la Memoria.

Archivo Prisma. 2023. AV-6114 [*Auxiliares de Noticias: Lohana Berkins Encabeza Una Protesta En La Legislatura*]. 01:58. https://www.youtube.com/watch?v=uDV996YItA0.

Brizuela, Miguel. 2004. "Primera Marcha Del Orgullo Gay En Salta." Archivos y Colecciones Particulares / CeDInCI. Fondo Marcelo Ernesto Ferreyra.

Comisión Interamericana de Derechos Humanos. 2018. *Avances y Desafíos Hacia El Reconocimiento de Los Derechos de Las Personas LGBTI En Las Américas*. No. 184. OAS. https://bibliotecacorteidh.winkel.la/Product/ViewerProduct/839#page=0.

Defensoria del Pueblo CABA. 2017. *La Revolucion de Las Mariposas*. Statistics. Defensoria del Pueblo de la Ciudad de Buenos Aires. https://www.algec.org/wp-content/uploads/2017/09/la_revolucion_de_las_mariposas.pdf.

Di Carlo, Cintia. 1986. Reclamo de Travestis En Plaza de Mayo. Buenos Aires. Fondo Marcelo Ernesto Ferreyra. https://sexoyrevolucion.cedinci.org/s/la-comunidad-del-archivo/item/5145.

Diario Crónica. 1971. "Hombres Vedettes 'Les Girls 71' (Suzy

Parker).” Fondo Editorial Sarmiento.

Diario Crónica. 1986a. “Revuelo: los travestis copan la Plaza de Mayo.” December 26. Fondo Editorial Sarmiento.

Diario Crónica. 1986b. “Travestis Hacen ‘Bis.’” December 29. Fondo Editorial Sarmiento.

Diario Crónica. 1987a. “Lloran a ‘Boquita Pintada’.” August 17. Fondo Editorial Sarmiento.

Diario Crónica. 1987b. “Los travestis de Plaza de Mayo acusan: ‘Sí nos quieren matar, moriremos en la Casa de Gobierno’.” January 20. Fondo Editorial Sarmiento.

Diario Crónica. 1987c. “Travestis ‘indignados’. Murió otro, arrollado en Panamericana.” March 8. Fondo Editorial Sarmiento.

“El Cronista Comercial, 14 de Mayo de 1992.” 1992. Fondo Marcelo Ernesto Ferreyra. Programa de Memorias Políticas Feministas y Sexogenéricas - CeDInCI.

F.D [Francisco Defazio] (Cámara Nacional Criminal y Correccional. Sala de Cámara. July 1966).

F.D [Francisco Defazio] (Cámara Nacional Criminal y Correccional. Sala de Cámara. December 1966).

Grandis, Gonzalo. 2021. “Se presentó la metodología del próximo Censo en la reunión inaugural del Comité Operativo Censal.” Censo Nacional de Población, Hogares y Viviendas, August 19. https://censo.gob.ar/index.php/se-presento-la-metodologia-del-proximo-censo-en-la-reunion-inaugural-del-comite-operativo-censal/.

Hanglin, Rolando, and Luis Santagada. 1966. “Los ‘ex’ hombres.” *Revista Panorama*, April. Archivo Histórico de Revistas Argentinas (35).

Instituto Nacional de Estadística y Censos - I.N.D.E.C. 2019. *Nuevas realidades, nuevas demandas: desafíos para la medición de la identidad de género en el Censo de Población.* Documentos de Trabajo 25. INDEC.

Julio Cesar Caram, dir. 2019. *Los Travestis y La Prostitución: Revelador Ciclo de Notas (1987).* 12:35. https://www.youtube.com/watch?v=u9MUTrnAfnI.

Larson, Sam. 1994. "Situacion Argentina." *Revista Ka-Buum,* July. Fondo Sam Larson. Programa de Memorias Políticas Feministas y Sexogenéricas - CeDInCI.

Monsú, Axel, and Daniel Tortosa, dirs. 2001. *Vanesa Ledesma Documental Trans Córdoba 2001.* Video, 16:57. https://www.youtube.com/watch?v=AQBJalCZJF0.

"Página/12, 15 de Mayo de 1992." 1992. Fondo Marcelo Ernesto Ferreyra. Programa de Memorias Políticas Feministas y Sexogenéricas - CeDInCI.

Prensa Obrera. 2007. "El Gobierno Ordenó a La Policía Que Espíe a Todos Los Que Apoyan La Lucha Docente." *Prensa Obrera,* March 21. https://prensaobrera.com/sindicales/el-gobierno-ordeno-a-la-policia-que-espie-a-todos-los-que-apoyan-la-lucha-docente.

Principles and Recommendations for Population and Housing Censuses: 2020 Round. 2017. Revision 3. Economic & Social Affairs. United Nations.

Revista Ahora. 1987. "Los Travestis Quieren Protegerse Detrás de Un Sindicato." September 3. Fondo Editorial Sarmiento.

Revista ESTO. 1987. "Falta otra 'niña' en la 'ruta cruel'." August 21. Fondo Editorial Sarmiento.

Revista ESTO. 1988a. "El lider de los travestis, sin pelos en la lengua." August 12. Fondo Editorial Sarmiento.

Revista ESTO. 1988b. "Sí te matan llamame por teléfono…" October 21. Fondo Editorial Sarmiento.

Revista ESTO. 1989. "Cuando Julio Sosa desafinó con el tango de la muerte." April 28. Fondo Editorial Sarmiento.

Revista ESTO, and Julio Fernández Blanco. 1987. "Los Travestis de Antes No Pisaban Panamericana." September 11. Fondo Editorial Sarmiento.

Revista Flash. 1987a. "El Travesti Deborah Singer Denuncia 'Han Matado a 4 Compañeros En La Panamericana.'" January. Fondo Marcelo Ernesto Ferreyra.

Revista Flash. 1987b. "Los Reclamos de Los Travestis Que Trabajan En Panamericana, Frente a La Casa de Gobierno." January 6. Fondo Editorial Sarmiento.

Revista Flash. 1988. "Un travesti denuncia que 63 colegas pasaron las fiestas dtenidos en cuatro comisarias." January 19. Fondo Editorial Sarmiento.

Revista Flash. 1989. "Actua, canta y baila pero le impiden presentarse en TV porque es travesti." June 29. Fondo Editorial Sarmiento.

Revista Libre. 1987. "Mónica es el Ubaldini de los travestis , quiere formare un sindicato y afiliarlo a la CGT." August 25. Fondo Editorial Sarmiento.

Sansone, Rosario. 2007. "*Entrevista Con Rosario Sansone.*" Archivos y Colecciones Particulares / CeDInCI ( Serie: Argentina, Subserie: General) Fondo Marcelo Ferreyra.

Urbina, Karina. 1996. "*Letter to Rosario LGBT Committee.*" Museum of Memory - Rosario.